# The Art of Open Relating~

*Volume 3*

## Trials, Tribulations, & Lessons Learned

Carl E. Stevens, Jr.

First Edition

ISBN: 978-1-7331648-1-8
Self-As-Source Publishing
Author: Carl E. Stevens, Jr.
Published: June 2020
Web Address: https://www.progressiveloveacademy.com

# CONTENTS

# ~ 0 ~

## Preface

*Preface*

THIS BOOK IS EXPLICIT and for grown folks only! If you have strong conservative beliefs around sexuality and relationships or strictly believe in monogamy and traditional forms of marriage as the only way to relate, then this book isn't for you.

This book is explicit with frequent uses of profane language and references. This book isn't for children or anyone under the age of eighteen.

This is my ego speaking, so please don't get in your feelings about anything you read here. I'm just trying to work through the complexities of the heart inside of romantic relationships. I'm trying not to hide from my inner vulnerabilities because they're certainly hard as hell to deal with. Nothing exposes my heart more than loving the feminine principle and being open and vulnerable to her. It's so powerful yet so sublime in how the feminine wields its power and influence. So beautiful.

Also, I know there are two sides to every story, and then there's the truth. If you asked my girlfriend's opinion on my stories about them, they'd probably say I was full of shit. I get that, which is why I'm saying this is merely a detail of my feelings, perceptions, and experiences - not the absolute truth. I'm sure I'm leaving out plenty of relevant details, but not intentionally.

These words are simply my raw experiences with women after Kenya (my wife) and I opened our marriage back in 2006. It's just an account of my experiences working through emotional challenges, having amazing sex, and learning how to manage the expectations and desires of multiple women simultaneously. That said, I don't hold back on the darker side of my experiences in some of my open relationships, either. There are too many relationships to recount here in this manuscript. I've selected some that are the most pertinent and relevant to the lessons I've learned over the years.

# THE ART OF OPEN RELATING

Once again, this book is explicit, so grown folks only.

This book isn't a how-to manual on open relating or open marriage. (however, I'm sure there are some valuable lessons to be learned within these pages.) This book is raw, vulnerable, and real. Read it if you want to hear honest accounts of some of my relationships as well as critical shaping factors in my life. For open relating steps and tools, read my book - *The Art of Open Relating Volume 1: Theory, Philosophy, & Foundation* published in 2018.

What makes this book unique is that I'm a married man who's in an open marriage, who doesn't hold back on his feelings and experiences. I live with my wife, have my own room, am the father of three children, and have dated and related with scores of women since becoming open. I've been talking about and practicing the open relating lifestyle for almost two decades.

This book isn't an indictment of anyone. It's not a story of regret. It's not about me evaluating choices and wondering, "What if?" I love my life. I created my life, and I wouldn't have it any other way than how it's unfolded. I'm not saying that I would make the same exact choices again, given the same opportunity, but I'm content and at peace. There are no victims or villains.

This is just a piece of my open relating story and journey.

Oh yeah, Rakhem Seku is my spiritual name and the one I prefer to go by with friends and partners, so you'll see it used instead of Carl throughout the book.

# ~ 1 ~

**PART 1: Youthful Folly**

ONE OF MY BIGGEST complaints about marriage is that people get married, but have no idea what marriage is actually about. There really should be courses on marriage that talk about the real deal, but I haven't seen anything like that out there.

The first part of Kenya's and my marriage wasn't bad because we were surrounded by a community of people who could guide us through the journey. They showed us some real-time examples of what happens in marriage and child-rearing. That wasn't the case, though, when it came to open relating. We had no guidance and no support. Everything we went through was us feeling our way through the dark. It's not like today where polyamory is a huge trend with support groups, coaching, books, and communities dedicated to expanding the practice. We started our journey before those support structures existed before open relating became more popular because of the polyamorous movement. For that reason, PART 1 of this book is called Youthful Folly, which is named after the fourth hexagram of the I Ching oracle system, which warns of the trials and tribulations that come from inexperience. Youthful Folly is what happens when you enter a new area of life without a teacher or guide, and that's what we experienced in the first stage of our open relating journey.

## How We Opened Our Marriage

I guess you could say that Kenya and I had a history of being radical and eccentric. When I met her, she was brash and bold, but also had a delicacy about her. I used to tease her about being this petite woman who'd be stomping through the streets of Washington, DC, with her black leather boots, long dresses, and leather jackets. She kind of came off as a tough girl, but she really wasn't. She was just a revolutionary who wanted to see change happen in the world. She would meet with her friends and type up newsletters to organize students on Howard University's campus to stand up for their rights. She'd write letters to the Department of African-American Studies to put pressure pushing for changes to the curriculum to better serve their students' needs of students in a highly segregated world. It was fun watching her work and motivating her friends to push harder and do more for the cause. She was also a part of an all-woman band called Soulfood Symphony that carried an equally radical and progressive message in their music. Kenya played the upright bass, which in and of itself was a sight to see. Here's this five-foot-four petite woman handling and holding up this heavy, dense, wooden six-foot instrument on stage and jamming it out. You would think that she'd be no match for it, but when you actually touch her body, you could feel the solid muscle from her lifetime training in gymnastics and dance. Her strength wasn't apparent when you simply looked at her structure, but whenever we had sex or fought, it was unmistakable.

We met on a blind date while we were both attending Howard University. She was getting her undergraduate degree in Education and Early Childhood Psychology, and I was getting my MBA. Two months later, we'd be engaged, and ten months after that, we'd be married. We had a lot in common philosophically, and that was the foundation of our connection. Our early dates would be us going out to eat every night and talking for hours about philosophy, religion, metaphysics, the state of black people, and diet. She had an incredible body and was super cute; especially, when she wore earth tone colored lipstick. My favorite was the matte maroon lipstick because it went well with her black eyeliner and concealer. It was a unique look, and all the girls in her band dressed similarly. Overall she was very conservative with her dress. Never showing legs or cleavage, but her beauty still showed nonetheless.

About a month after we were engaged, we joined a spiritual community, which became the foundation for a lot of the work we'd end up doing together later in life. We had a reading done with a set of Kemetic (ancient Egyptian) oracle cards to determine the purpose of our relationship and what energies we would be relying upon to make things work. We found we had a high spiritual calling. We would eventually be married by a polygynous family - one man and two women. They gave an amazing service and speech to the community in attendance, which included family and friends. The fact that they were polygynous became a slight distraction for some of the folks there. However, it did not prevent anyone from enjoying the wedding festivities and showing their support to Kenya and me.

Our marriage was mostly "normal" compared to society's standards. We were your standard monogamous couple and started having children soon after our wedding. What set us apart was our very strict and very conservative spiritual community. It was considerably different from other mainstream religions. We went to full moon rituals at nine at night and didn't leave until about three in the morning. We wore whites or whatever the color of the lunar cycle was. We were strict vegans, used oracle cards to make our major decisions, and would possess the ancestors to get insights on what moves to make next. When you came to our house, it was full of shrines from the door to the bedroom. I guess those things might seem extreme, but it's really no different than what you would find in any other religious household where there are spiritual altars and ornaments all around the house.

Everyone has their traditions and activities that they practice as a part of their culture and religious practice. Ours was just something that didn't fit the dominant religious beliefs of most people. That's all. I still worked in corporate America. I'd wear my slacks, khakis, button-up shirts, and sit at the computer for most of the day. Everything else was normal except maybe me meditating at lunchtime in an empty conference room.

The spiritual community we belonged to allowed polygynous marriage, which was one man married to many women. The leader of our community had about four wives at the time that we joined, but that number would change often. It was also hard to tell who was who because women would be in line to be a part of his family, and then nothing would happen. It was kind of like following a soap opera to see what was going to happen next. Polygyny was basically a lifestyle afforded to the men in leadership positions. None of the other men would ever be successful in obtaining other wives, but it was fun as shit watching them try. Most men would just settle for cheating on the low or leaving the community all together if they wanted to get some other pussy. Usually, when you got caught cheating, you were put out of the community or at least had to go through a long, arduous counseling process to get "fixed." It was comical when I look back at it now because all of the men were in competition for the best looking women, but again, the men in leadership positions would usually have their first pick of the litter leaving the rest of us to dream about the possibilities.

We had a brotherhood where all the men in the community would come together to learn about masculinity and spiritual concepts. We also organized all the work that we had to do for the community - and there was a lot of it. Our community operated a school and a grocery store, and both businesses needed to be cleaned every night. Things had to be moved around. We also did a lot of events that required things to be moved and security to be present. It was endless, really. We did a ton of work in the name of building the community. It was a great experience for me. I really feel like I developed more into a man during that time in my life because of all the examples of manhood I had around me. I'm talking about married men with multiple decades of experience with their wives, plus children they were raising. It was great to get marriage advice from them, and just hearing their stories and perspectives was amazing. It was well worth all the work that we had to put in. Some of the men had multiple wives, and that was interesting as fuck too, just to hear what they had to share and their perspective.

One of the big topics was how to maintain a high level of sexual vitality. We would talk about holding your semen during sexual intercourse, what herbs and vitamins to take to increase our virility, and how to circulate energy and not deplete ourselves. We'd talk about how to manage women and how to show up in a supportive way for our wives. Truly amazing discussions and information. That was basically one of the things I loved most about being in the spiritual community - bonding with the other brothers in the men's group and getting shit done together. The entire experience was dope, but the fellowship was number one for me. One of our favorite topics was how to go about getting multiple wives, which was funny because all of us were struggling with the one wife that we did have. We were all getting beat the fuck down by marriage and having a hard time managing our wives. Plus, I really felt that our women were in a mode where they were hypersensitive about their husbands trying to add additional women to the family. It's like they couldn't ever relax for fear of their husbands bringing someone else home or requesting the elders to add another wife. It was funny because the women would act like they were open to it for the sake of being in line with the community, but none of them were. The only women who were open to polygyny were the women who weren't married yet. Even the single men were trying to figure out how to get multiple wives, and you could look at them and tell they weren't anywhere near ready. No jobs or money. Low maturity levels. No patience. No sexual skills. It would have been a mess. The good thing about the community was we were all subject to counselors. Meaning, before you could get married or do anything significant in your life, you had to go to counsel about it. Everything required a reading, and it required a level of approval for you to do it if you were serious about being a community member in good standing. That was a great thing because it prevented the men from just adding wives to their families or from jumping into marriage when they weren't ready.

There was a sister in the community that I wanted to add to my family. I wanted her to be my second wife. Why? First of all, because I wanted multiple wives and second because I was sexually attracted to her. Third of all, because we had gone through a tough time when Kenya was dealing with ovarian cancer (trophoblastic's disease), and she needed to be on chemotherapy. It was a rough time for her and our family because we had just had our oldest son Senbi and had to rely on the community for support. Kenya had to start chemotherapy two months after Senbi was born, which meant she couldn't breastfeed him anymore. That was a major blow to her as a mother and to our family because we firmly believed in being holistic when it came to raising our children. One of the things that I appreciated about that time was having other women in the house to help out with taking care of Senbi, cooking, cleaning, and being a friend to Kenya in general. In my mind, going through that time with other women supporting seemed to offer logical proof that polygyny was beneficial. Even outside of a major illness, it seemed logical that numerous women in the house had significant benefits. It was this experience that really pushed me into a strong desire for polygyny.

I didn't mention polygyny until years later after Kenya had recovered. I talked to Kenya about it, and she wasn't down with it but agreed to go to counsel about it. Both she and my counselors were in attendance during our session. When they asked what we were here for, I said, "I'd like to add Zalina to the family." It was funny because they already knew what I wanted to do, but wanted to hear me say it. They asked Kenya what she thought about it, and she said, "I don't think we're ready." They said ok and proceeded to do the oracle card readings. Their counsel was to wait until year ten of the marriage and then come back and ask again. We were in like year three of our marriage. I was pissed as a moutherfucker, but Kenya was happy as a six-year-old on Christmas morning. I've never seen her that happy before or since. She looked at me and said, "That sounds reasonable right, Rakhem? That makes perfect sense to me." I just looked at her with disdain in my eyes but kept my mouth shut. That was the thing about having a counselor - we were obligated to follow their advice. It's not like we were just relying on their opinion and experience, but also the fact that they were doing readings with oracle cards on everything we inquired about. I'm sure if the cards looked more favorable, they would have considered giving us the go-ahead on polygyny. Maybe I should revise the "us" and say, give "me" the go-ahead. I still doubt it, though. I'm sure they could see Kenya wasn't down for it just like they could see I was a little too eager to make it happen. In the I Ching oracle system, they call that Youthful Folly when you don't have the experience to know what you're getting into. Looking back at it, not getting their approval was probably one of the best things that could have happened to me. Knowing what I know now, that polygynous union would have ended in disaster. I'm so happy we didn't go through with that, and I'm thankful for the checks and balances that we had in place to keep our relationship on track.

So, I guess you can say that our open relating journey began in that counseling session where I tried to move my family into a polygynous structure, but it's more complicated than that because we had another consultation a few years later about another matter that you can say was related as well. Kenya was having orgasmic dreams about Abin Sur, the lead djembe drummer in our community. She was dreaming about him at night and having orgasms in her sleep. She was also deeply attracted to him. One day she approached me about it and said, "I can't stop thinking about Abin Sur." You know how you hear or see something, but it's so foreign to your frame of reference that you don't even really process it? It's almost like I didn't really hear what she was saying, like her words were a ghost. In my head, I was thinking, "What did she just say?" It didn't feel wrong or icky, but just foreign. I asked her, "What?" She said, "I've been dreaming about Abin Sur every night for the past few weeks. I'm kinda obsessing over him." From one standpoint, I could kind of understand it because all of the women in the community were attracted to the drummers. In African spiritual culture, drummers are like DJs or the lead singer in a band. They are usually really vital men who carry a lot of masculine energy. Most of the time, they're drumming for hours at a time, holding the rhythm and keeping the women on the floor inside of a deep trance that has them dancing and moving spontaneously. We're essentially talking about a warrior energy that dominates the room even when they're not inside of an actual ceremony. Djembe players use their hands to hit the drum, and the good ones can drum fast and with tremendous force. When their hands hit the drum, you'd think their hands were made of steel or something. It'd be like "POP! POP! POP!" I know this well because I would later become a drummer in my community as well, but I would play the djun-djun, which was a much larger drum that you played with wooden sticks.

I never really viewed Abin Sur as being overly masculine, though. He was about five feet, four inches tall, and had a very soft-spoken manner about him. He wasn't "not masculine," but he wasn't the stereotypical lead drummer either. He was a really good guy. He was married to a dimepiece, but they would later divorce due to internal marital strife and infidelity.

As a side note, it's interesting seeing people reject the concept of open relationships only to later end up in divorce, with hatred for one another and broken families. It's like, don't you see that monogamy isn't working for you and that there's possibly another way to do this relationship thing?

When Kenya brought this to me, Abin Sur was still in a stable marriage (as far as we knew) to his wife with two sons who were the same age as my two oldest children. We would eventually go to counsel - Kenya, her counselor, my counselor, and I - to discuss the matter. Kenya explained to them about her dreams and that she was in love with Abin Sur. The counselors did their readings and advised Kenya to just forget about the whole thing. Ignore the dreams and focus on your husband and family. That seemed like the safe counsel to me. But at the time, I really wasn't even comprehending what was happening. Like, it was hard for me to grasp that my wife was actually in love with another man. We left that session with a directive, but no clarity.

But it didn't end there. Word got back to Abin Sur about Kenya's feelings. Apparently, it caused some strife within his household, which led all of us back to a counsel session – him and his wife, Kenya and me, and all our counselors. All I remember is that Abin Sur's responses were basically a series of shrugs and "I don't know what she's talking about" type statements. Abin Sur's wife was deafly silent during the entire session, which was only matched by my silence. Again, we left the meeting with directives, but no resolutions. When Kenya and I would talk later, she insisted to me that Abin Sur could somehow feel what she was feeling too. She thought he must have been in touch with her dreams and could feel the energy, but was ignoring those feelings because of his wife and situation at home. Kenya is insistent about it even to this day that he could feel what she felt, which wouldn't surprise me because Kenya is highly intuitive.

I didn't know much about Abin Sur's wife except that she was a dimepiece. I mean, she was drop-dead gorgeous. She had a natural symmetry about her face with beautiful lips and smooth brown skin that was undeniable. I remember when they got together and announced they were getting married. He got so many props from the brothers for securing a total dime. I didn't know much about her because she was eerily quiet most of the time. She would speak and laugh here and there, but she kept mostly to herself. There's a saying about watching out for the quiet ones. Well, that apparently applied to her because behind the scenes in the marriage, things were rougher than anyone realized. But that wouldn't come out until over a decade later.

I can say, from that time on, it made my relationship with Abin Sur a bit weird. We were never really super tight, to begin with. Still, we were brothers in the same community and both members of the brotherhood. He wasn't as active as me, but we would often end up doing work together and being around each other a lot. One of the things that made our relationship interesting is that my oldest son turned out to be an amazing drummer. He had skill and rhythm that was astounding for his age. The master drummer Mamade Keita had a chance to hear Senbi drum in one of his classes at only the age of three years old. He said, "I've been all around the world, and never have I seen a child so young with so much talent."

I really needed Abin Sur to be a guide for Senbi because I just wasn't a drummer (at that time) or musically inclined. I really couldn't guide him in a way that he needed. Abin Sur's son was also a drummer, and he had the benefit of being around his father to help him develop. It was awkward because I felt that there might be some competition when it came to our sons. Also, the weirdness of Kenya's attraction to him was always playing in the background. I mean, it's so weird to have to go to counsel about someone being attracted to you. Usually, people just fuck on the down low and keep shit as quiet as they can. Who knows - maybe if Kenya would have approached him secretly, they would have hooked up. Then the weirdness would have only been on his end because I would have been none-the-wiser.

It's all speculation now, but the point is that I really could have used his support during that time with Senbi, and I never really got it. It's like, if we knew about open relating back then, maybe we could have just been cool with him and Kenya having a relationship. That might have strengthened the bond between us all. I can't even imagine what the energy was like between him and Kenya because she believed so strongly that he was feeling what she was feeling. Was their interaction awkward, or was there some anger there? I don't know. I was attracted to his wife, so maybe, well, you know. Maybe she was attracted to me too.

The bottom line is that things could have turned out differently. I often wondered if their marriage could have survived if they were able to be more open and honest about how they felt. The fact that Abin Sur went on a massive cheating spree with another woman from the community kind of tells me that he very well could have had an attraction for Kenya. If so, he was burying it probably because of not wanting to deal with another man, me, in the picture. The woman he would eventually cheat with was single at the time, and they fucked all over the city. It was one of the more infamous cheating scandals in the community, partly because of his high profile as the lead drummer in all of our rituals and the fact that his wife was a dime. It just makes me wonder if we could have tackled that situation differently what the potential could have been.

There's so much potential if human beings could learn to come together and work together in various ways. I mean, every situation doesn't necessarily hold the same promise, but when you see families fall apart like that, it just makes me wonder sometimes. It makes me wonder if anything could have been done to work things through. Open relating as a relationship modality itself could have saved the family. But, obviously, both spouses would have to be amenable to trying something new and changing their beliefs, which is no small task.

## 5104

The next leg of my open relating journey was interesting. It occurred when my family was living communally with four other families in Washington, DC. You see, in the year 2000, our house burned to the ground. We owned a single-family home in the Takoma Park neighborhood of Washington, DC. We were about one block from the subway station on a dead-end street.

We bought the house right before the real estate market blew up in the city. But the house burned to the ground on Christmas Day of 2000. We weren't there because we had left to go visit Kenya's parents the day before. The official fire department report said the cause was a wire that was wedged between the basement door and the floor, but I thought it was some candles that we left burning on the Sebek shrine.

My next-door neighbor actually caught the fire on videotape, but I never got a chance to see it. We were at Kenya's grandparents' house when we got the call from Ur-Aua-t. She said, "Just relax and breathe, Rakhem. Ok? I've got something to tell you." I thought it was super weird that she would call us on Christmas way up in Port Huron, Michigan, which is about five miles from Canada. She continued, "Your house caught on fire and was damaged very badly." I was thinking to myself like, "What the fuck?!" There are certain bad feelings that we experience in our lives, but your house burning to the ground is beyond all of them. I've lost my wallet, keys, had my car stolen, and gotten the news that Kenya had cancer and would need to go on chemotherapy. But hearing that your house has burned to the ground, that all your belongings are gone, and that you have nowhere to live is a serious gut punch. The good news is that we weren't there. The bad news is that we didn't really have the maturity to handle the aftermath of that situation. It's hard to explain, but we never really recovered from that event. It's mainly due to a series of missteps on my part, but I guess you live and learn.

We ended up staying in several different places while trying to work out getting the house rebuilt. Eventually, we ended up staying with another family in the community who we had a lot in common with us in terms of our goals and objectives. Both of our families were interested in living communally with other families "on land." Meaning, we wanted to have some acreage that we could live on and practice a communal, holistic lifestyle. That was the dream. Instead of focusing on buying a place right away as a group, we agreed to live together first to see if we all got along. The concern was whether or not we could manage our many different personalities under one roof. Two other families who were also interested in the same communal vision would eventually move in. Altogether, there were eighteen people under one roof. My youngest son was born in that house in December of 2003.

It was a great living dynamic and one of the best living experiences of my life. There were four adult males, three adult females, and eleven children of different ages, from infants to teenagers. It was great to have men to bond and connect with in the house. It felt like a true brotherhood, and all of the men were mature and hardworking, so we got shit done when we needed to. It was also cool for the women to have one another to bond with to share duties and support one another. But the best part about it was the children having each other to play and bond with. It was the infamous "self-check" in basketball where you don't really have to guard a particular player because his offensive skills are so limited he couldn't even score if he was on the court all by himself. Living with children communally was like that for me. They watched each other and took care of each other. As adults, all we had to do was get them to and from school, feed them, clothe them, and be their primary support network. I loved it. It made me want to have more children. I even wanted up to eight at one time. That's how good it was to raise children in a communal setting. That said, I'm so glad I didn't have more children because it's a grind I wouldn't wish on anybody.

The dynamics in the house were good. We did rituals together at night, shared chores, split the costs of things when we could, and shared other resources as well. We would support each other with issues and problems as they came up. But some interesting dynamics came up while we were all cohabitating together, and those dynamics revolved around sex and relationships. It's true that we were all a part of the same spiritual community and that the community believed in polygyny, but that belief didn't address the types of challenges that came up.

For example, early in the process, one of the couples living with us had a falling out. I believe there may have been some cheating going on, and the husband would eventually leave the house. This is how we got down to three men in the house instead of four. This left the wife and her two children with no intimate male presence. On the other hand, the fourth family was really just one man who moved in as a solo addition to the house. He was casually dating other women but didn't have any committed relationships or partners throughout his entire stay at the house. That made the housing dynamic as follows: My Family - Kenya, me, and our three children, The House Owner's Family - Husband, wife, and four children, Family Three - Wife and two children, and Family Four - Solo Man. We had a few other people float through here and there, which is how our numbers got to eighteen, but these four family units were the foundation of the house.

On a side note, the spiritual community we were a part of was pretty bland when it came to sexual expression. We were no different from any other standard religious organization where sexuality was basically suppressed. That is, there was no room to even acknowledge other attractions. So that's the background. Major sexual suppression and repression in effect.

It was kind of an open secret that the Owner Wife liked me

and had an attraction to me. She would do little flirtatious things, but on a very, very subtle level. Nothing overt or obvious. It's the kind of stuff that has you in your head wondering what just happened. As a man, you're thinking, "Is she feeling me?" On the flip side, I had a real attraction for her. I can't even tell you what it was exactly, but I would have loved to get in that pussy. I felt that she kind of knew that, but again, there was no flirting on my part and nothing overt happening.

One day, I'm at the sink washing dishes, and she comes over to me and says, "You did a great job with dinner tonight, Rakhem. The kids really liked it." I said, "Thanks. I try to make good stuff, just like you do on your cook nights." Then she kind of leaned over to me and said in a soft whisper, "Why Rakhem? You'll never get this." I was like to myself, "WTF did she just say?!' I just turned and looked at her face, which was about one foot away from mine and looked at her. She looked like she was in heat or something. I thought about kissing her right there, but that would have gotten me excommunicated from the community, which basically happened anyway because of another unrelated issue.

It had me in my head trying to understand what the fuck she was talking about. Women are always talking in code and subtleties. I decided in my mind that she wanted to fuck me and that she was basically saying that I had to figure out how it was going to happen. I wonder how that would have affected our brotherhood in the house - me fucking the owner's wife on the low. Actually, she was the owner of the house. It was her name in the deed. Her husband came in later after her divorce was finalized from her previous marriage. Either way, no thanks. I was attracted to her and wanted the pussy, but not bad enough where I was willing to be the ultimate infidelity poster child. I mean, that's some low down shit right there to fuck the man's wife who is your boy and who has your family living in his house. But on top of that, I wasn't a cheater. I had never cheated on any woman, let alone Kenya. I wasn't even thinking about cheating. In our culture, when you're attracted to a woman, you add her to the family as a wife. There's no need to cheat on the low, though there were plenty of people in our community who did. If you're attracted to a married woman, then you just forget about her and move on. Basically, suppress those feelings.

But the big shocker to me was the way the attraction dynamic played out. I wasn't really expecting what happened. I wasn't expecting to be attracted to the sister and wanting to fuck her while I was in the house. I wasn't expecting her to say little flirty shit to me, either. You just don't think about those types of things when you're trying to do something of a higher order or greater magnitude like create a community on land. I guess it just caught me off guard.

It doesn't end there, though. Kenya was basically the best looking woman in the house. She was this petite thing with a fat little ass wearing the tight lapas. One day, we had a meeting about allowing a young lady to move into the house. She was single with no children, but she was attractive. I don't' think she was exactly down with the land project, but she wasn't against it either. After the meeting, the male owner said, "Yeah, it would be nice having some new blood in here. You get tired of looking at Kenya all day every day." I was like, "What the fuck did he just say?!" Oh, so the brothers are checking Kenya out like that. They're attracted to her and probably desiring her sexually. I mean, I kind of knew that, but to hear it was an eye-opener. It kind of made me look at my attraction to his wife a little differently. It made me think that there was a sexual tension that existed in the house in general, but one that we couldn't talk about.

21

It doesn't stop there, though, because we had a single woman (separated) and a single man living in the house. Everyone was thinking that they should just hook up. She's living by herself in a communal house listening to me and Kenya fucking and the other couple fucking, and I'm sure she's horny as hell. Her room was across the hall from ours. She was stupid thick with beautiful brown skin. All the men in the house wanted to fuck her, but there was no structure in place to allow that to happen. The single brother didn't want to have sex with her. First, he wasn't that attracted to her. Second, he didn't want to get forced into a relationship or marriage because the community was so strict and conservative when it came to sex and relationships. So he just left her alone.

One day the brothers had a meeting down in the basement about her. The owner started out by saying, "Someone has to fuck Reema." I just looked at the single brother like, "It's gotta be you, man. No one else in here can do it because we're married and our wives won't go for it." He's like, "Nah, I can't do all that, but I agree that she needs to get fucked and soon." We could all just feel the sexual energy coming off of her because that was her vibration. She was beautiful and sexual, and her vibes were affecting the house. It was making the men uneasy enough to have a freaking meeting about it. It may have even been affecting the other women in the house too, but I don't know how exactly. What came from our meeting? Nothing. No one volunteered, so things stayed the same with sexual tension in the air, affecting the house in God knows what ways. Look, I don't know the science of sexual tension, attraction, pheromones, and how all of that affects other people, but we definitely felt something. That's all I can say.

There were teenagers in the house as well. One teenage boy

and two girls. Umm...ok. So, what was going on with them? Were they feeling any of the sexual energy? I would say yes. How could they not? The house we lived in was a big Victorian house, but we were still kind of tight for space. It wasn't a mansion with multiple wings. We were sharing bathrooms and everything. I don't even know all of the attraction dynamics that were playing out in the house, to be honest. I can only speak from what I experienced and felt, and all I know is that it was there.

One morning Kenya and I were fucking in our room when I thought I saw something out of the corner of my eye. I was on top of her giving some long strokes. So I raise up higher to check my surroundings, and I see the teenage boy lying on the floor listening in on our session. I'm like, "What the fuck?!" I had to yell at him to scram, which he did expeditiously. I finished fucking, of course, and then went to address it with his parents. Talk about awkward from that day forward. I'm like, you all need to get this boy laid or something. See what I mean about the sexual tension in the house? I can only imagine what the teenage girls were feeling.

The house eventually disbanded. We came really close to buying a property and moving there together, but we couldn't agree on financial structural issues concerning ownership. Although we were close as a group, I believe our inability to address the sexual tension and needs of everyone in the house hindered our ability to be even closer. We were all good people, but we had things we couldn't really talk about. At least that was the case for me. I couldn't tell Kenya that I wanted to fuck Owner Wife. If Kenya wanted to fuck someone, she probably didn't feel comfortable telling me either, Especially after the Abin Sur debacle, in which the counselors basically told her to bury her feelings. I couldn't tell Kenya that Reema needed some sex and that I was going to provide it to her as a duty to the house. Where they do that at? I'm not saying these issues aren't complicated; however, they needed to be addressed in some way that's realistic and effective.

I left that situation feeling like our community didn't have the tools it really needed to address some of the core issues facing couples and families. We were dealing with feelings and energies that were above our pay grade. Things that people usually just handle on the low without the knowledge of their loved ones. We always looked at ourselves as an elevated group, just like every other spiritual and religious society does. Sadly, our limitations were definitely exposed during this situation. It caused me, for the first time, to start thinking beyond polygyny and monogamy as the only acceptable communal and relating structures because I had seen that both were limited in what they could address.

## Corporate America

After leaving the communal house and the spiritual community, I went back into Corporate America. I started working for my old company again, except this time I was traveling every week. I had to stop being a vegan because I wasn't getting the sustenance I needed to deal with the kind of travel and work hours I was confronted with. I would be gone for a week at a time in either Atlanta, Dallas, or Colorado Springs and would be with Kenya and the kids on the weekends. That's when Kenya and I would try to make up for lost time sexually. She was so incredible at having the house completely immaculate when I got home and having great ambiance in our bedroom. Kenya's sex drive was so high that there was no question about what was about to go down for the weekend, starting with Friday night.

Sometimes the sex was great and other times, not so great.

The truth was, I was usually tired as fuck when I got home from those road trips, and I wasn't getting back to the house until around nine-thirty at night anyway. We did the best we could, but I knew that it wasn't enough for her. She was losing patience, and what made it worse is that our sex life wasn't that awesome, to begin with. We had actually gone to counsel about our sex life and how she wasn't satisfied and how my frequency was low. Our counselors assigned me herbs and vitamins as a means to help out, but none of that stuff really worked. The bottom line is that my energy was super low, and Kenya and I weren't super aligned sexually. I mean, the sex was amazing, and she was highly skilled. She was also more cerebral than I wanted for me to have a super high attraction and desire for her. On top of that, I was usually a giver in bed, but I really like to receive. Left up to me, I would be a lazy lover in the bed to start out with and then put in my work in the second half of the session. Kenya liked to be ravaged and pursued more aggressively. She was also willing to continue as long as the energy was reciprocated, which most of the time, it wasn't from me. So it was tough because neither one of us was getting our needs met. One day Kenya came to me and said, "This traveling stuff is too much Rakhem. You're either going to have to get a new job, or we're moving to Atlanta, where you're working the most." She was tired of being at home by herself with the three kids and tired of not getting the sex and intimacy she desired. Plus, she was homeschooling our children too, which was stressful as a motherfucker. She also just loved having me there as a comfort, but with me traveling, it was like she was living as a single mother. Eventually, we would move to Atlanta as a family, and things would get better.

We were also able to get our sex life on track, too, thanks to working with a tantra master named Shantam Nityama, who taught us to expand our field of play when it came to our sexuality. Kenya did her research and learned to have full-body orgasms as well as squirting orgasms. I got more into and effective at eating pussy. I started to practice energy work on her, which allowed her to have orgasms without me touching her, and our sex life got much better. It wasn't one-hundred percent fixed, but we pretty much hit the peak of where we could go as a couple, which was pretty good. Before, she would only have clitoral orgasms, but now she was having all kinds even before I penetrated her. For the first time, we were being mindful of whether the neighbors across the street could hear us having sex or not. That is saying a lot because we were living in an Atlanta suburban single-family house in a neighborhood with plenty of space between homes.

While I was working in Corporate America and traveling around the country, something major happened to me that had never really happened to me before; I fell in love with a woman. It was a strong pull that I had for her, and it was different than anything I had ever felt before. It was different than my connection and attraction to Kenya, which was more of a feeling of pure love and appreciation rather than a feeling of being deeply in love with her. This was a draw and a pull. The woman happened to be a coworker of mine, and it totally caught me off guard because she wasn't what I was used to being attracted to physically. She was kind of homely, very down to earth, dressed very conservatively, and was a little nerdy. This was a super huge shock to me. I just couldn't believe how badly I wanted her. The closest feelings I've had to the love for her were the feelings I had for another woman (Diamond) inside of our community several years earlier.

I didn't want to add Diamond to the family because she was much younger, and I didn't feel it would be practical. Not only that, but she would get married soon after that, so I just kept my feelings to myself. We ended up being just really good friends at that time, and our children would end up being friends as well. Even though my feelings were super strong for her, I was able to suppress them pretty easily. I was basically able to do what our counselors told Kenya to do about her feelings for Abin Sur. It was easier for me because I didn't see any way that she and I could be together. Her joining our family wasn't practical, and I wasn't going to cheat on Kenya. I had always been against cheating because that's what happened to my mother when I was growing up. My biological father cheated on her, and she found out and divorced him. She actually found him in a restaurant with another woman when he claimed that he would be out studying at the library. It crushed her. I remember when she came home after seeing him in the restaurant and just collapsed on the floor right when she got in the house. My biological father eventually arrived and tried to console her, but it was a mess. A total shitshow. I was immediately ordered to go to my room. They would be divorced soon after. My step-father entered my life less than a year later. He took primary responsibility for raising me, which is why I refer to him as my father. His presence in my life wasn't really a traumatic experience for me because of the respect I had for him. Having to deal with my biological father was rough because everything was so forced and tense between him and my mother. But the bottom line was that ever since that experience, I wasn't willing to cheat on a woman. Every time I had a girlfriend, I stayed loyal to her. All the women loved that quality about me. Looking back at it, it wasn't necessarily the best thing based on my reasoning. Meaning, I was still suppressing feelings instead of dealing with them head-on. Either way, it worked for my situation with Diamond.

At this point, we're still living in Virginia, right before we moved to Atlanta, and I brought my feelings to Kenya. I told her I was in love with my coworker, and Kenya immediately wanted to meet her. I was still in the polygynous frame of mind and wanted to add this woman to my family. Kenya didn't freak out because she literally brought the same thing to me about six years prior. We would all end up going out to dinner one night, just the three of us. It felt a little bit awkward, but it went surprisingly well. Kenya just wanted to check her out to see if she was a realistic threat to our marriage. Her determination was absolutely not. She didn't see my attraction for her other than her infatuation with me. What's interesting is this young woman would have been willing to join my family. I honestly believe that she would have been down for it. Why? Well, she was originally from Ghana and migrated here as a young girl, so she's seen that type of thing before and had family members who practice polygyny. I think she also would have done it because she was super attracted to me. I was at the manager level at my job, was responsible, and had a ton of potential to advance within my company. I'm sure she would have felt comfortable following my leadership.

But again, I wanted this woman bad and wasn't really willing to take no for an answer. I was determined to add her to the family, and guess what? We weren't a part of our spiritual community anymore, so there would be no readings or counsel to fuck things up this time. Checkmate. We discussed this for several months until Kenya would ask a profound question that would change the course of our relationship dynamic. She asked, "What if instead of you adding her to the family, we both date other people, Rakhem?" I was just like, "What the entire fuck did she just say?!" I was like, "Hell, fucking no!!" I couldn't believe she had the audacity to even let those words come out of her mouth.

I had never heard of something so crazy before. Where they do that? On what planet does a married woman date other men? What's that even called anyway? She's totally lost it. Either way, we were at an impasse. If Kenya couldn't date other men, then I couldn't add another woman to the family. This sucks! This shit is like deja vu.

Kenya and I would continue to debate the concept of open relating for about two years after that. I wasn't down with her having sex with another man. It was so far outside of my level of understanding and world view that I couldn't even visualize something like that happening. I couldn't even get to the point of jealousy around it because it was like a foreign language or something. I guess part of the challenge is I've never seen an example of something like that before. I've seen a man with multiple women, whether openly in a polygynous union or on the down low in a cheating scenario. I think I may have heard about women cheating on the down low, but never really saw anything in front of me. Like, I never had homegirls who would break the game down to me about how to have multiple men or how to get over on their husbands. I just wasn't in those circles. So when Kenya talked about having multiple men, it was totally foreign to me. I just didn't have a frame of reference to even judge it or evaluate it. All I could really do was reject it out of fear of the unknown.

Later, I would be introduced to how prevalent women cheating on their husbands actually was. When I started dating Edrea, I would hear a ton of those stories. She worked for a psychic hotline, and most of her callers were married women who wanted readings on how to get more time with their boyfriends. It was a total shocker to me to hear it first hand, and no, these women weren't in an open relationship. They were monogamous, married, and with a boyfriend who was usually younger than them who they really wanted to be with full time. No, they weren't fucking their husbands at all and didn't care how their husbands felt. All they cared about was getting their new guy. All these women had jobs and were making money. It was from my other girlfriend that I found out what the husbands were doing for sex, intimacy, and attention. They were going to sex workers and massage parlors. My other girlfriend - The Craziest Bitch on Earth - was a sex worker, and ninety-five percent of her clients were married men who were cheating on their wives. These were married men paying for all kinds of sexual services while on business trips and otherwise. Anyway, it just gave me a full view of what takes place in many monogamous marriages, but I was glad to get first-hand information on the women's activities as well.

## Tantra

I mentioned before that Kenya and I took the time to fix our sex life. We did it through the study of tantra, which is a study around broadening the power and impact of sex through the expanded application of energy. We had studied some tantra early in our relationship, but didn't get into it too heavy until we met Shantam Nityama, who was a tantra master from California. He was able to show us how to manipulate energy to affect our auras and physical bodies to the point where we could have profound levels of pleasure and even orgasm. For us, this changed the game. We were able to work with him in a few different settings and eventually began practicing on our own. What he showed us was so profound that I was very open to what he had to say about sexuality and relationships as well.

We learned about the qualities and characteristics of feminine energy. This was critical for both of us because no one else seemed to know anything about the actual energetics of gender. I learned so much. I realized I was wrong about so many things about what the feminine was, and conversely, how to show up for the women in my life.

One day, we were all sitting around the table talking at our house. We had invited Shantam to our house to lead a three-day retreat and demonstrate and teach his specific brand of tantra. He said something so impactful and profound that it opened the door for me to consider allowing Kenya to have partners in the same way I wanted. He said, "You can't cage women or feminine energy. You have to allow women to be with who they want, when they want, wherever they want. It's the only true way to honor the feminine." That statement fucked my head up. The way I read it, he was saying that women had to be totally free to be in their feminine energy and that caging women by restricting their movements or relationships was a violation of their ability to cultivate their femininity. I determined that I was basically caging Kenya by not allowing her to have other partners while desiring that reality for myself. It was so funny how I couldn't even see the inequality in what I wanted. It took those words to allow me to open up to thinking more rationally and reasonably about sexuality and relationships.

Soon after our three-day retreat, Kenya and I would agree to open our relationship, that the next phase of our relationship would begin at that point, June 8, 2008. From that point on, we would do the very best we could to be honest and forthright about our feelings for other people and what we desired. We also agreed to leave the past in the past. We would not rehash anything we had gone through up to that point, including all the arguments, debates, or any perceived transgressions that we put on one another. It was literally a fresh start.

## Going Forward

The remainder of the book is about some of my experiences after opening my marriage with Kenya. I've included not only descriptions of the relationships, but the lessons and trials I've had over the years as well. It's essentially my recollection of some of the most impactful experiences that ended up shaping my current, but ever-changing relationship philosophy.

So, let's start there. What is my relationship philosophy when it comes to open relating as of the date of publication of this book? When I say relationship philosophy, I mean how I actually operate within my relationships.

# ~ 2 ~

## PART 2: My Story & Open Relating Philosophy

We all have a relationship philosophy that we follow. That philosophy defines things like standards, boundaries, expectations, goals, and the foundation for our specific relationship ethic. PART 2 of this book explains where I am at this time in my relationship philosophy. My philosophy was formed based on the events primarily in PART 3, but also the preliminary events in PART 1.

But before I can get into my philosophy, I need to tell my story. We all have a history that explains who we are and what events shaped our growth and development as human beings moving into adulthood. While it is true that my adult relationship experiences shaped who I was and how I viewed women, the childhood events laid the foundation for my entire life. These events would affect every aspect of my life, including my initial relationship philosophies. So, I start PART 2 by telling my story.

# My Story

I was lying in my bed, but I wasn't asleep yet. Just an average school night that was topped off with a cold bowl of cereal and me curling up in my full-size bed. My mom and "biological" were out doing whatever it is that they do at night time. My brother was in his room asleep. I always marveled at the way he was able to go to sleep, no matter what was going on around us. Well, he was four years old, so maybe that had something to do with it. He was always the first one asleep in the house.

Whenever my parents were out in the evening, I would usually stay up until one of them got home. I think it was just a comfort thing. I wasn't scared to be home alone with only my younger brother because everything felt safe and familiar in our suburban neighborhood.

I'm lying in bed one night when I heard the front door burst open, and a something hit the floor with loud thud. I immediately jumped out of bed and ran to the top of the stairs. My mother was sitting on the floor with her hands in her face, crying uncontrollably. I started to rush down the stairs to help her because she seemed hurt in some way, even though I couldn't tell exactly what was wrong with her. When I get to the bottom of the stairs, I ask, "Mom! What happened? Are you ok?" She barely looked up at me and told me to go back upstairs and get in bed. That was so confusing to me because it was obvious she needed help. "Carl, just go to bed." I was still confused, but I started to walk up the stairs slowly and head back to my room. When I got to the top of the stairs, the door burst open again, and this time it was my "biological" rushing into the house. He immediately started talking to my mom. "Jo. Jo. Let's talk, Jo." My mom's name was Joann, but he called her Jo. Then, all of a sudden, he saw me at the top of the stairs watching everything and said, "Go to your room, Carl."

I took a few more steps up the stairs and then looked back to see what was happening. They were arguing. Now my mother was standing up, and they were in each other's face. Tears were still streaming from her eyes down her face, though. My "biological" had his usual stoic look on his face, but there was an intensity to it. I think I got his stoic facial expression features because people say that I'm stoic too. Things started to get heated enough that I knew I needed to take my ass to my room. I got in my bed as I continued to hear the commotion happening downstairs. The noise would eventually move upstairs, but it all just became a blur to me.

36

I had never seen them fight like that before, except once when he might have struck my mother. It was in the afternoon, and they were arguing in the kitchen. She had him in the corner, yelling at him about something. That's when he lashed out in what looked like a hit to the face, but I couldn't tell. Whatever it was, it was enough to get him out of that corner, which he did promptly. Other than that, I can't remember any big fights or arguments between them. That would change though after that night because the next day, I realized they weren't going to be together anymore. I remember him grabbing his stuff and leaving the house. I don't think he said anything to me at the time. I don't think there was much commotion, either. It was just him moving expeditiously to get out at my mother's request.

From that day on, every interaction I would see between them was hostile. It could be them on the phone or in person or her just talking about him. It didn't matter. Never a kind word. Never anything said in peace, compassion, or happiness. It was strictly venom from that day forward, especially from her. It was my first lesson in seeing how fucking pissed a woman could be at a man for literally the rest of her life. I'm almost fifty years old now, and I've seen forty-three years of venom spewing from her towards him practically nonstop. It's been incredible to watch and behold. I would have never believed it was possible if I hadn't seen it with my own eyes. He had his own venom that came out as these sly jabs and barbs at her, but it wasn't anything too extreme. He was just mostly in a perpetual state of defending himself.

But from that day forward, all I remember is saying to myself that I needed to step up and be the man of the house now. That my mother needed support and someone to fill my biological father's shoes. I can literally remember telling myself that, and I could remember my whole demeanor changing as well. Like, I could feel it in my blood and bones that I was now the man of the house. I wasn't going to be a child any longer. I wasn't going to be someone who's getting in trouble at school or giving my mother problems. That day shaped my persona for my entire life going forward as well as all the meaningful choices as well.

I would wonder if that night not only affected my inner child, but also my relationship with my younger brother. He slept through the entire thing, by the way. I'm watching my mother and "biological" end their marriage in grand fashion, and my brother was sound asleep. He was only four years old, but it's interesting to remember how that event affected us in different ways. I always felt that he was affected more by the divorce, but in hindsight, he was just affected differently. He wore his emotions on his sleeve and showed challenges in school and socially as a result. Nothing super major, but enough for my mom and me to notice. I was apparently alright because I never caused any problems for my mother. In retrospect, I was covering up some things that needed addressing.

My brother and I were never really that close. We really didn't bond that well, and even in our adult years, we never really talked a lot or kept in touch as much as we should have. It was weird because my brother was my favorite human being on the planet (next to my grandfather on my mother's side). I loved how my brother seemed to have the basics of life in order. He was always ahead of me on the foundational side of life. He was married before me. He had children before me. He established his career in the military before my career took off in the corporate world. I loved his family and marriage, even though things wouldn't end well there. I loved his relationship with his children even after he and his wife separated.

He was kind of my idol to a degree, but I would never tell him that. He's the younger brother, right? I'm the older brother and the one responsible for him and for holding the family together. But I think my attitude of stepping into adulthood at an early age may have separated me from him to a degree. It's like, we weren't two children anymore. We weren't brothers anymore. I was the guardian, and he was the child who needed support. It's not like I did anything that was guardian-like, though. I wasn't actually taking care of him or anything. It was all in my mind. I can't help but think that it may have caused a strain on our relationship. Only God will know, I guess.

So there I was - a young boy looking to prove his worth by being the "good" man who always did the right thing in the eyes of his mother. It's how I judged myself, and it's how I looked for love from my mother and, eventually, all women. Rakhem, don't be your "biological." Be better; be noble; be nice. Don't hurt her or any woman for that matter, and maybe, just maybe, you'll be worthy of calling yourself a man and receiving love in return. That's what I created in my mind and eventually through my behavior. That was the carrot on the stick that I would chase from age seven until age fifty. The only challenge is that I didn't know I was chasing that carrot until I was almost fifty. I guess spiritual growth and development truly is a journey. I think life is about finding the real you, pursuing your true purpose, and finding peace within, based on what's illuminated on that journey.

My life would continue on. My mother would meet my father. The man who actually raised my brother and me. The man who has supported us always in every way, even until today. He was super solid, but I still felt like I needed to be the man and step up, so I continued to be nice, good, and do the right thing. My mother was a teacher and eventually a principal in the same district where I attended school. That added even more pressure on me to never get into trouble or make her look bad, which I never did. All the teachers knew me and knew who my mother was, so non-compliance was an impossibility.

When I was in middle school, I wanted to be like the top athletes because they got all the girls. If you weren't a top athlete or a part of the super cool clique, then you got no parts of the pussy. It was dry as fuck. I played sports - football, basketball, track, and soccer, but I was never a top athlete. Why? Because I was too fucking nice. I would get that message from my coaches throughout my middle and high school years. I remember one time, we were running a drill where one person runs down the field with the ball, and the other person tries to tackle him. It was a one-on-one drill and supposed to be hard on the defender because the field was so wide it would be challenging for him to actually tackle a ball carrier in the open field. I remember when it was my turn to run with the ball, I ran in a zigzag pattern down the field, but I was making slow progress because I wouldn't commit to actually running up the field. I was running more horizontally than vertically. My coach got so mad that he chased me down and tackled me his damn self. I remember looking up at him when I was on the ground, and his face was super red because he was so pissed. When he got up, he yelled at me and the team and said, "That's how you commit to something and be aggressive! We aren't playing patty cake out here! This is football!!!" That would be my last year of football.

I also remember when we were playing basketball, we were running a similar drill. One guy had the ball and had to dribble past three sets of defenders who were stacked all the way down the court. But the trick was you only had about ten feet of space to work with to get by the defenders. The bleachers were on one side, and the rest of the team formed a line on the other side. When it was my turn to get by the defenders, I would only get by one of them before getting crushed up against the bleachers when trying to get past the second line. I ended up losing the ball and failing the drill. Next up was this young player who was a grade behind me, but he was tough and built like a tank. He ended up getting by all three lines of defenders and completing the drill successfully. That drill cost me my starting position as the point guard for the team, and I was replaced by the younger guy. My coach, Mr. Hanks, would always preach toughness, but again, I was the nice guy. I didn't have the killer instinct that I needed to compete on a high level. I didn't have that fuck it attitude where I would put everything on the line even if it meant hurting or injuring other players.

The interesting thing is that my dad was a super tough guy. He was built like a rock because he was a boxer when he was in the army. He carried guns and was quick to fight anybody. Even though he came into my life at the age of seven, I never got his aggressiveness. I never got his fearless attitude, but instead continued to play the nice guy.

When I started dating girls in college, the women on campus wanted me to come and talk to their boyfriends about being faithful (i.e., being nice). They all liked the fact that I didn't cheat on any of my girlfriends and wasn't afraid to preach faithfulness and being a good guy at every turn. Their men hated to see me coming because they knew they were going to get a lecture from Mr. Goodie Two Shoes. I'm sure they hated me, but I didn't care at that time. I was still on a mission to be the guy who doesn't cheat or hurt women under any circumstance. I was living my life for my mom, and being the man my "biological" could never be.

I was happy with who I was and the fact that I had a perfect record when it came to being faithful to the women I dated. I carried this record into marriage, but my Nice Guy demeanor would eventually come back to haunt me because I started to realize that I couldn't get what I wanted and also keep everyone happy. I first started to see this in Corporate America where I noticed that my supervisors were very cut-throat in how they negotiated with clients. They were also tough on employees who were under their leadership. As I started to move up the ladder, I found it harder and harder to be the nice guy. One day, my supervisor Troy pulled me aside after a call with a client and said, "You've got to tell them what they're giving you is unacceptable. You've got to get tougher on them and stop trying to keep them happy all of the time. You've got to have balls when you get to this level. Things aren't going to be pretty in negotiations, and you're going to have to accept that if you want to be successful in this business." That was a wake-up call like a motherfucker. All of these messages throughout my life were the same.

I would eventually start running away from conflict again. I would leave my job twice to pursue entrepreneurial opportunities, but the same lessons followed me there. You can't be a nice guy in the entrepreneurial world, or you'll get eaten alive. I lost tens of thousands of dollars. Lost deals and eventually lost my shirt. I was left with nothing. My family was homeless for a time and then in and out of temporary housing. All in the name of not cutting throats and trying to keep everyone happy. Don't get me wrong - my wife was pleased to have a faithful husband who was positive and a good guy, but we couldn't sustain a lifestyle that would take care of us and our three children.

It wasn't until I would fall in love with another woman that I realized that I could no longer get what I wanted and needed and still keep everyone happy. That's where the rubber hit the road for me. Yes, I tried to get another woman to join our family by going to counsel with the elders when we were in spiritual culture, but when that failed, I was still left wanting without any alternatives. I was going to have to confront the woman I loved most - Kenya - to get what I wanted. I was going to have to face and offend my family and her family to get what I wanted. I was going to have to battle for over a decade to stand in my truth because I had denied myself for so long trying to be someone that I wasn't.

I remember Kenya saying to me one day, "You went to college to be an engineer, but that wasn't what you really wanted to do. You were following a path that you thought your mother wanted for you and not what you really wanted to do." When she told me that, I didn't fully accept it. It was too early in our marriage for me to be open enough to deal with that truth. Plus, it was hard for me to see myself doing anything other than what I had done - go to college, go to graduate school, get a job, get married, have children, and live happily ever after. It was the only path that seemed right. It was the path that my "biological" failed at, but one that I would get right to prove to the world that I was worthy.

The open relating journey is where I would find the supreme confrontation in my life. It's where I would find the most rejection. I was relentlessly attacked online for my lifestyle and beliefs. My manhood was attacked. I was called a simp and a cuckold. I was called morally depraved, especially after appearing on numerous television shows. Kenya would do a blog that talked about her open relating journey, and that officially made me the bad guy in women's minds. They saw me as backing Kenya into a corner and forcing her to be in an open marriage to keep me in her life. It was a rough time. But it was also the start of my freedom journey.

This is my story.

# My Open Relationship Philosophy

When I look back at a time when I was free to be myself and live my life without the input or pressure of others, it's been clear that I've always lived an open life. During my first year in college, I got no pussy. Or let's say very little and the pussy I got was from women no one was really checking for. These were nice women with great personalities and really good hearts, but they tended to lack swagger and appeal. They weren't into makeup or clothes and hadn't learned the feminine art of magnetism, which is all the young men my age were into back in the day. I went to summer school after my freshman year, and things started to pick up a little bit, but things were still scarce in the woman department.

In the fall of my sophomore year, I pledged a fraternity and became an instant celebrity within my peer group. But I had met a cute young lady and decided to be with her as soon I completed the pledging process. We had a great relationship. She was my college sweetheart. We were supposed to get married upon graduation, but things didn't work out because I went into depression when I couldn't find a job. We got together twice while in school. Once after I finished pledging Kappa during the fall semester of my sophomore year and then again during our final year in college together. We ended our relationship the first time the summer before my junior year started, and I was officially on the market.

My junior year was spent having more sex and with more partners than I could have ever imagined. It was the most sexually active time of my life. It would remain so until I opened my marriage twenty years later. After I settled down a bit and got comfortable in my powers to talk to women, fuck women really well, and maintain solid connections with them, I would keep a rotation of about five to six women at a time in my circle. I would just kind of rotate them each night, which amounted to seeing them about once a week each. Sometimes it got tiring, but it also felt really good having that combination of variety and consistency in women. What I had found was basically my natural relating balance with women. I loved the stability of the structure combined with the diversity of the women. This felt like my ultimate calling.

Obviously, I wouldn't stay in this type of relating structure because I would end up getting married and being sexually exclusive with my wife, Kenya. Not only was I exclusive with every girlfriend I ever had when I was in a committed relationship, but I never cheated. I felt that separated me from the average man out there in the world who couldn't seem to stay faithful to his girlfriend. Women would always ask me to talk to their boyfriends or invite me to parties so I could hopefully lecture the men about staying faithful. I was happy to do it, but it's not like it was going to help them keep their dicks in their pants. It was deeper than that for them. They had a programing and set of supporting beliefs that told them cheating was the standard in monogamous relationships. And guess what? They were right. That's basically the standard behavior in monogamous marriage - cheating, deceit, secrets, etc. It is what it is.

What's interesting is that monogamy might have worked for me if I played by the rules of cheating on the low. Then again, I wasn't good with deception and the stress of maintaining those kinds of secrets. It stressed me out, to be honest. I'd rather just stay faithful to my woman rather than turn myself gray and bald, trying to maintain multiple secret relationships. Additionally, I also had the childhood trauma of seeing how my biological father cheating on my mother affected her emotionally. Seeing her pain and anger prevented me from being able to do that to any woman I was connected with. As I mentioned earlier, the women I dated loved that about me, and, in retrospect, it wasn't necessarily a good thing. Setting a standard for yourself based on childhood trauma isn't something to be proud of because: (1) it's not sustainable and (2) it's not being done authentically or for the right reasons. You should choose sexual exclusivity only if it aligns with your rationality and principles.

I wouldn't return to this lifestyle until I opened my marriage in 2006-08. That's when I slowly started to date multiple women again. It happened naturally, too. All I did was react organically to the attractions and connections that presented themselves throughout my normal life. The beautiful thing about women is they will let you know when they are interested in you. They'll give you that look or come over to you and flirt or just start a conversation. It's such a shift from that "chase and pursue" strategy that I thought men had to do. It's so much better to let the women be the choosers in relationships, and then for me to be the pursuer once that choice has been made.

Now I find myself married for over twenty years and dating scores of women at a time, and it's beautiful. It's one of the happiest times of my life, to be honest. Women are so beautiful and magical and sexual and nurturing and giving and insightful. I love it and I love human connection even though I can be reclusive at times. What makes my lifestyle even better is that I can just be me without having to pretend to be someone else or sneak around on the down low. What a fucking relief to stand inside your truth for all the world to see. Does that mean everyone knows all my business? Fuck no. I keep things private that I need to be kept private. I still protect my personal brand from the opinions and critiques of the masses whenever I can because no one has time to try to explain themselves to a bunch of people who are just looking for a reason to tear you down as a way to deal with their own unresolved pain or unhappiness. Certain relationships and connections require discretion and privacy, especially with husbands and boyfriends who are oblivious to what their wives are really doing. Or maybe these men aren't oblivious at all but are satisfied with her doing her thing as long as he can do his thing. Who knows? Monogamous culture is weird like that where sometimes the relationship is based on an "as long as I don't see it, it's ok" type of unspoken agreement. All I know is I let women tell me what the deal is with her man and I act accordingly. "Do you have things in check or not?" Or better yet, "Call me in a few years when you have things under control at home, and you've learned to manage your man and relationship. Your shit looks a little too volatile."

I'm now dating up to thirty women each year. The main question I get is, "How do you manage all of that Rakhem?" Like, where do you find the time? Do they know each other? Is there a main woman? Do they know your wife? Do they get along with your wife? What if they want more from you, and it infringes on another partner's time? Does your wife like your partners? Can your wife tell you not to date someone you really like? What if your partners have children? What do you do for protection from STDs? How do you avoid pregnancy? Have you ever gotten a partner pregnant? What if she wants to keep your baby, but you don't want to keep it? Would your wife leave you if you got another woman pregnant? Can any of your partners stay with you in your house with your wife? Do you help partners with bills? Do you have threesomes with your partners? Do their husbands or boyfriends get mad at you? What if one of your partners wants to get legally married to you? Are you willing to divorce your wife and marry her? Can your wife do what you do and you be ok with it? What are the rules of engagement between you and your partners? What about holidays, anniversaries, birthdays, and Valentine's Day? Do you rank partners? How does a woman get the title of girlfriend, partner, or life partner? Once they get that title can they lose that title? Are your partners allowed to date other men and women or do you put restrictions on them? Have you ever fallen in love with one of your partners and wanted to be exclusive with her? How would you tell your other partners if you wanted to break up with them to be with another partner exclusively? Do you do long-distance relationships? How do you have time to date all these women, Rakhem? Do you see a moral conflict in your lifestyle? Are you a religious person? How does your lifestyle align with the word of Jesus Christ? Why not just be single Rakhem? What is your definition of marriage? Do you think you will ever leave the open relating lifestyle and just settle down with one woman? Is this lifestyle fair to other women considering you know they want more from you? Rakhem, you do know these women really want exclusivity and a family from you, right? Does your wife just put up with your lifestyle because she doesn't want you to divorce her? How does your lifestyle affect your children? Do your parents know about your open lifestyle? What's the end goal Rakhem? What good can really come from all of this dating? Isn't this just about sex? Do you actually have love for these women? Have you considered getting a psychiatric check-up Rakhem to ensure you're not channeling unaddressed mother issues? How many women have you hurt through your lifestyle? Would you consider the women who date you to be of low self-esteem and self-worth? Do you feel that some women just use you for sex until they find their long-term partner? Do you date men Rakhem? Don't you have to be less of a man to allow your wife to date other men, Rakhem? Have any of your partners actually fought each other? Have any of your girlfriend's husbands confronted you? Where do you get enough sexual stamina to have sex with all of these women? When does it end Rakhem? What happens when you can't physically fuck any more Rakhem? Who's going to take care of you then? Who Rakhem?

These are amazing questions. I have answers for all of them, but they don't all need to be answered, partly because the point isn't to answer them all. The point is to give you enough of an understanding of my relationship philosophy so that you can see who I am and how I approach open relating. The other point is to show how the complexity of open relating not only raises some very valid questions but also creates havoc in your life if you're not in the right mindset to manage things. In other words, you have to be about that life as they say.

That said, let's see if we can answer some of them now to give some context to my open relating lifestyle. How do I manage all of the women I'm dating? I guess the real question is, do they really need to be managed? I really only need to manage my time and my energy. Meaning, I can't get into overpromising my partners what I can and can't do more than I can physically and emotionally sustain. In the end, I can't treat my relationships like exclusive, ownership-based relationships because to be with multiple women, I must be free to move about the country as I please. In traditional monogamous relationships, it's expected that constant communication and accountability for your movements and actions are made available to your partner. This is understandable because that one person is providing all your needs and desires, but that's not the case with me. I'm not a "primary" partner to any of my girlfriends. They all know that (a) I have a wife and live with her and (b) that I date multiple women, freely and openly. Therefore don't have the time or energy resources to act in an exclusive manner with them. I'm not open relating because I want to replace Kenya with another primary partner. I'm open relating because I value living my authentic life and organically connecting with women. In short, the expectations for me in my relationships are much different than what you would find in a traditional monogamous relationship.

Even in polyamorous relationships, you find they tend to mimic a series of monogamous relationships. You might have two or three primary partners instead of just one. That means you're dedicating exclusive energy to each of your partners, but to a lesser degree than you would if you were monogamous. I guess the best way to view it is that polyamory can sometimes look like polygyny, but with the freedom of your partners to have other partners as well. That's not how I live my life. I'm into organic connection, freedom of expression, and a dedication to me taking personal time for myself. As a matter of fact, that's the best benefit of open relating for me - taking time to just be by myself. I really enjoy my "me" time, and I enjoy not feeling obligated to break my solitude if it's not what I want to do. The only exceptions are, of course, responsibilities like children, etc., but those begin to fade as we enter our later years. My wife and I have been married over twenty-four years, raised our children, and gotten past many of the obligatory child-rearing responsibilities that used to capitalize our time.

Do my partners know each other? I would say they know of each other partly because they all met me through my work, which is relationship coaching and teaching. So, many of them are or were part of the same community, people interested in the principles we teach at our school. From there, we all know women talk and are expert investigators. They find each other or meet in the cyber world or whatever. Are they friends or associates? The smart ones aren't. They simply keep it at knowing one another without trying to befriend each other. I really don't push my partners to be friends or know each other or interact or communicate in any way because there's really no point to it. I mean, me being a common partner to two women isn't enough of a foundation to sustain a friendship, let alone a sisterhood. For some reason, people think it is a foundation for friendship, but trust me, nothing can be further from the truth. Plus, nothing good will come out of it because all of my relationships are different. I spend more time with some partners and do certain, unique things with others. The universal knowledge of that among my girlfriends would only lead to comparisons and jealousy. I'm not from the school of forming some big community or living in some massive compound together. It's just not my thing. I have zero interest in anything that resembles polygyny. I have zero interest in managing women's emotions in a group setting or helping everyone get along.

I admit that I did have that dream a long time ago, but that was before I actually had experience dating multiple women as a married man. I'm so glad I didn't go the polygyny route when I was younger. Kenya and I actually went to counsel about forming a polygynous union with some other women who were a part of our community. Our counselors told us to check back in with them after ten years of us having been married successfully in a monogamous union. I'm so thankful and grateful for our counselor's wisdom because that would have been a dumpster fire. I wanted to do that back in my vegan days, and I didn't have even half of the sexual drive and stamina that I do now almost twenty-five years later. And to think that the woman that I wanted to add to our family had a sex drive through the fucking roof. Add that to my wife's super high sex drive, and I wouldn't have made it. Fights, arguments, and eventual divorces would have followed. I'd rather my partners make their own choices and relate and befriend who they'd like, and while they do it, take full responsibility for those friendships. I don't want any calls from one partner saying another partner isn't speaking to them or whatever. It's none of my business, so please handle that yourself.

All that said, I've had a number of my girlfriends get together and become friends, but I really haven't seen it work out. Usually, what will happen is that a woman who is interested in me will befriend one of my existing partners as a way to get to me. She'll ask questions, be her friend, and get her support in talking to me, but it always ends where they hate each other. Why? Because the friendship wasn't based on anything real between them. It was based on me, which isn't a good foundation for a bond between women. My thing is if you want to be friends with someone, make sure it's for the right reasons and that you all really and truly do like and love one another. Anything else is folly.

Do I have a main woman? I guess you could say my wife Kenya is my main woman because she's the one that I've been through the most with. We've been married for over twenty-four years, had children together, started a business together, went through spiritual initiation together, opened our marriage together, and grew our characters together through our relationship. That's a lot of history and to still be friends and to still love each other is saying a lot. We're not together out of obligation, but because we both desire it and see the benefit in our marriage. Unlike other monogamous couples, we both have other options in front of us every day to be and live with any of our other partners at any time. It wouldn't be a problem at all. We'd just make the adjustments and support each other in the transition. Other than my wife, I would say that my main partners are the women who are providing the most loving support in my life at any one time. I'm more of a form-function kind of guy. The question is, what are we doing for each other right now. Yesterday was great, but today is where it's at. Are you in my life, supporting me, loving me, helping me get through each day, or do we just see each other when time permits? Are we soothing and supporting each other regularly or not? That's my measure for the "main" woman. So I guess I do have a main woman, but it's not a static reality that never changes. One thing that my marriage has taught me is that consistency and longevity matter. It counts. So I see how my connections and relationships unfold over time and determine which ones are my primary relationships and can withstand the test of time.

So they know of each other, but I don't promote interaction. Do they know my wife, Kenya? They all know who Kenya is. There isn't a woman I've dated since opening my marriage who doesn't know who Kenya is, what she's about, and her overall philosophy about open relating. Are they friends with her? Not usually. Not if I have anything to do with it. You have to understand that there's a lot that comes with being a wife. There are a lot of emotions, ideas of how things should be, and a lot of comparisons too. As my wife, Kenya will have the natural reflex of attempting to dictate things. This will include my partners, as well. If my partners befriend her, Kenya will naturally and organically wield her influence over them and subconsciously pull the wife rank thing in her interactions with them. I'm not even saying it's malicious or intentional. It's a remnant from monogamy where the wife expects to have the final say over certain of her husband's interactions. It's natural, and for that reason, I'd rather not have my partners interacting with my wife. I'm not with them so that I can have an extension of my wife's influence creeping back into my life. I'm with them because I want to enjoy a unique relationship that is purely reflected in only our two energies coming together. I don't want my partners trying to think like Kenya or doing things that are going to make her happy because that might not be what makes me happy. I've had numerous women befriend Kenya as a way to get to me, and it usually doesn't work out well in the end.

Kenya and I have two different philosophies about how we practice open relating. Kenya is more communal and hierarchical, and I'm more of a separatist and circular in my arrangements. Meaning, Kenya wants everyone under one roof singing Kumbaya, sharing responsibilities, living together, loving together, but where she's ultimately in charge. Um, no dice. Women who have tended to align with Kenya are the ones I tend to stay away from. It's like dating her all over again, and the energy doesn't flow freely and easily. Their consideration of what Kenya says and does is always playing out in the background and it defeats the purpose for me. Does Kenya get along with my partners? Sometimes. She's usually cordial at least and sometimes can form solid connections with them. I don't stop that when it happens naturally. That said, Kenya's views on whether I should date a particular woman never comes into play. I'm open to her opinion, but she has no veto power over any of my partners. I would never stop dating someone because Kenya demanded me to unless it was an extreme circumstance or some serious disrespect was involved.

A number of my partners have children, and I think that's great. Every time I'm with them or around them, I treat them with respect and basically like they're my own children. I don't discipline them or get too bossy, but my intention is to be a solid adult figure in their lives. I've done a lot with some of my partner's children including taking them to track meets, giving them rides, giving them money, playing games with them, talking to them about life, helping them with school work, encouraging them to play with my children, talking to them about dating, working out with them, and the list goes on. Really, my goal is to be a friend and stable figure in their lives. That said, I've never been someone who is a high-frequency interactor with my partner's children. Meaning, I've never tried to position myself as a replacement to their biological fathers. In my view, that would be the wrong message. My relationship with my partner's children should be unique and specific to us while avoiding mimicking any other relationship.

To that point, my partners have been free to interact with my children at home too. My children have met and interacted with some of my girlfriends over the years. It's worked out well from my point of view. I've had girlfriends cook for my children, do hair, play with them, give them rides, do music projects, take them shopping, give them gifts, talk to them, watch movies, babysit them, counsel them on school and business, and the list goes on. I expect all of my girlfriends to just be solid, caring adults around my children and get in where they fit in. There's never a need to feel squeamish or hesitant around my children. If I'm dating you, it means you have sense, and I trust you to interact with my children.

What about my philosophy on sexually transmitted diseases and pregnancy? It's funny how these two topics are often discussed in the same conversations. My philosophy is it's my responsibility to protect myself from disease in the best way I can. That means doing what I feel is the best thing for me to do. At the same time, I'm interested in my partners also being protected and want to keep them out of harm's way in any way I can. I would expect that they would do the same for me. However, it's not their responsibility to do so. That responsibility rests purely on me, just like their protection ultimately is on them. For example, one of my younger girlfriends insisted that I get tested for sexually transmitted diseases before we had sex. I obliged her, and my report came back clean. When she came to visit, we had sex without a condom, but she also still wanted me to wear a condom for most of our experiences. I was in total agreement with her desires and obliged her because she's doing what she feels is best for herself. It's her responsibility to protect herself, and she's got to take the steps she needs to do just that. In another instance, I ended up having sex with a cutie who was working at a fast-food restaurant. Although I don't usually choose to wear condoms, I wore one with her when we banged in the back seat of her car. It just depends on how I feel and what comes out in our conversations around sexual safety. After she and I talked, I decided it was best.

What about pregnancy, though? That is something that had been one of my bigger fears since my college days. My mother insisted that I use protection while I was in school as a means to avert pregnancy. She basically told me that my life would be over if I ended up getting a young lady pregnant while in college. The result was me wearing condoms almost religiously while I was in school. It wasn't even a disease that I was worried about as much as the possibility of getting someone pregnant. I still have some of those fears even today, but nothing like back then. For me, it starts with communication with all my partners about the fact that I don't want additional children at this stage in my life and not wavering on that fact. After that, it's agreeing on the kind of birth control methods we'll use when having sex. For some women, it's utilizing a long-term birth control method. For others, it's merely tracking their cycle to know when they are fertile. I tend to not relate with women who don't have knowledge of their cycle or who don't utilize some kind of birth control. It's just my preference because I'm trying to not wear condoms or pull out before ejaculation.

What I've also encountered is a number of my girlfriends have their tubes tied (tubal ligation), and some have had hysterectomies. To be honest, I prefer women who have their tubes tied. It usually means that they have already had children, gone through that experience, and are one-hundred percent certain they want no additional children. They also made the decision about no more children before they met me. I wasn't a part of their decision-making process to get the tubal ligation in the first place. Tubal ligation is a body altering-process, but it doesn't involve hormones. I've thought about getting a vasectomy, but I am not convinced that there are no side effects as men age; especially, in the area of erectile performance. That's just my fear.

Have I gotten any women pregnant since being in an open marriage? Actually, let me change the wording to better represent the collective decision of two people rather than place the blame on one person. Has a pregnancy ever resulted from sexual activity with one of my partners? Yes, pregnancy has occurred in a few of my relationships. In those cases, we mutually agreed to terminate the pregnancies either naturally or surgically. Abortion isn't the best feeling in the world or something any woman (or man, for that matter) wants to go through. And yet, I've always felt comfortable that the women who've chosen to abort a pregnancy did so because they thought it was the best decision for them. I support a woman's right to choose what she wants to do regarding her body.

That said, I also make it clear with each partner what my stance is on having additional children and what I perceive my role would be in case they did choose to bring a child into the world. I would definitely be in any child's life that I co-created. On the other hand, I won't be moving in with the mother, and I most likely wouldn't be sexually active with the mother going forward. It wouldn't make sense for someone who doesn't want children (me) to continue to have sex with someone who obviously does, based on their decision to bring a child into the world. It's nothing personal against her, but I believe in being with women where there's a philosophical alignment; especially, when it comes to something as big as children and family. One of my personal philosophies is that raising children is a major responsibility and takes one-hundred percent commitment to be done the right way. It goes beyond just having two parents in the household because that's not even enough, in my opinion. It really takes two parents who sincerely and authentically have a desire and love for parenthood. Like, each person has to have a passion for being a mother or being a father. I believe that is the essential combination that raises children and allows them to have the love and attention they need to thrive in their development. I believe this combination is also critical in children growing up to be psychologically and emotionally balanced. It is also what's required for the parents to remain psychologically and emotionally balanced as well.

I believe one of the biggest causes of divorce comes from the psychological wear and tear of raising children where the parents aren't one-hundred percent bought into the process.

Meaning they "wanted" children but really didn't have a passion for motherhood or fatherhood. The resulting stress of the ordeal became something that would tear the marriage apart, although it would appear to be something else like lack of love, lack of communication, financial problems, or cheating. No, it was the stress of the daily, relentless grind of raising children that contributed towards one or both partners stepping out in search of pleasure or relief. Or it's the shame of being unhappy raising children that doesn't allow the open, honest communication between spouses that could allow for problem-solving and open dialogue. Or it's the change in the mother's vagina or object of attraction that no longer has her attracted to her husband after giving birth. I remember when Kenya told me about how my scent changed after she gave birth to our first son and how her attraction standards changed after birth. She said she literally looked at me differently, and it wasn't because I had done something different. It was all triggered by the process of having children. Being passionate about parenthood can help with keeping an open dialogue during the natural and inevitable ebbs and flows of maintaining a family. This is just my observation over the years, but I know folks have a hard time discussing the realities of childrearing because it's taboo in our modern culture to say anything other than loving, positive things about the experience. So I can totally see how others wouldn't see it my way. Still, I make sure I let all my partners know my stance on children without romanticizing the experience. This has been a big challenge with some of my younger girlfriends who maybe don't have children or only have one. They just don't have enough experience to have a realistic frame of reference to make an assessment. They're still seeing the cute baby pictures online or the baby food commercials, and it's making them want the fantasy without regard for the reality. It's all good, though, because I was the same way. As I stated earlier, I wanted up to eight children when I was living in the community, so I totally get the desire.

These are important conversations to have because they do come up in the open relating arena. These things need to be dealt with just like anything else, and I've done my best to honor myself and my partners throughout these discussions and trials.

Do I think Kenya would leave me if I had a child with another woman? Absolutely not. Kenya loves community and babies. She would try to integrate that partner and the baby into the community in some way. Not that she would want to live with the baby, but she would acknowledge it and treat it like a member of the community. I would do the same thing for Kenya if she had a child with another partner. I would respect that child in the same way that I would if she had that child already before we got married. I wouldn't be that involved in raising the child, but I would support Kenya in the best way I could without dishonoring my freedom and relationships with my other partners. If I had a child with another woman, I wouldn't bring that child into the house with Kenya. It's not my preference to do so, and I wouldn't burden her with that responsibility. I also wouldn't bring the mother of that child around for the same reason. It would just be too much overhead, and I don't want to expose my children to something that is potentially heavy or traumatic. As I've said, I prefer to keep my partners separate, and the same would go for a situation like this.

Even outside of having children, I wouldn't bring any of my partners to live in the same house with Kenya and me. First of all, I've already done that, and it was a disaster. Second of all, I don't want to overlap relationships. Again, it's just too much to manage, and the return isn't worth it for me. Multiple women in my house isn't appealing to me in the least mainly because I like my alone time. I don't see that happening with multiple women under the same roof. I'm not saying it's impossible, just highly unlikely. I've never seen that scenario work before with one woman, let alone multiple. No thanks. Plus, like I said, I'm not trying to manage a bunch of emotions, pettiness, and bickering over shit that's just not important to me. Trust me, I understand why men say they want to have multiple sexually exclusive women under one roof, but these are usually men who've never done it. Similarly, I've several partners who wanted to move in with me, but again, in most of those cases, they've never done it before. We'd be talking about one big experiment which is almost guaranteed to end up in a cluster fuck.

I think what makes that fantasy appealing for men is the idea of doing threesomes with all his wives in the house or something like that. I'm not interested in threesomes and never have been really. Have I done them before? Yes, but it's not really a big deal outside of being able to say you've done it. I prefer one on one interaction with my partners because it increases the intensity. I like to focus on one person. That may go against what people think I'm into, but dating multiple women isn't synonymous with threesomes or wanting to be involved in fringe sexual encounters. No shade against threesomes or people into that, but it's just not my thing, so no, I don't do that with my partners. If they asked me to do it, would I? Maybe. Like I've said, I've done it before with partners, but it's nothing that I seek out.

I feel like I need to acknowledge the source of my feelings when it comes to not wanting to live in community or engage in polygyny with Kenya. Some of my feelings are based on times when I've had other women living with us. Some of those experiences were traumatic events for me, and I really don't want to go there again. The same goes for polygyny when I say I don't want it. I really don't want that kind of set up with Kenya, and at this point in our relationship, it's not even an option. We're both fully open at this point, and there's no way Kenya would go to a polygynous situation with me. I highly doubt she would do polygyny with any man at this stage in her life. All that said, Kenya is not the only factor influencing my views on polygyny. Like I just said, I wouldn't want to manage the emotions of multiple women under one roof. I've observed other polygynous families as well, and I've judged that they don't really work. I've judged that the women are underfucked and trapped in a situation that can't feed them on a soul level. I see the men as not being fulfilled because, just like in monogamy, the sexual magnetism and polarity diminishes, and they are no longer sexually fulfilled by their wives. As a result, they go out looking for additional wives to spark the sexual fire again, and the cycle continues, leaving the original wives with the same unmet desires, but without any outlets or alternatives.

Nonetheless, I believe that polygyny could work for me, given the right partners and circumstances. My girlfriend Monie Love said she believes that I'm really polygynous at heart. She said, "Rakhem, you're really possessive. I think you're a polygynist." I agree with her that I can be possessive with the women I'm dating, but the level of possessiveness varies from partner to partner. I've never viewed my possessiveness very high with Monie, but it was extremely high with Bella, Diamond, and Erin. When I say "possessiveness," I'm really talking about my levels of jealousy and insecurity around my partners dating other men. I link all of that to levels of "in loveness." I think they're synonymous with one another - jealousy, insecurity, possessiveness, and the degree to which you're in love with someone. That said, I'm sure I could do polygyny or a version of it. It would have to be one where the women could be sexual with each other and where each woman was truly dedicated to me, such that being with me provided a level of fulfillment to help them exist inside a polygynous structure. The same goes for living in community. I'm sure I could do it in a community of the right women. That community probably would not include Kenya. There's a philosophical difference in how she and I would deal with that relationship structure as well as not wanting her to adversely influence my other partners. It would have to be a community that was structured on a philosophy that I vibed with. Hopefully, that clarifies my stance on polygyny.

One of the most interesting criticisms I get from women outside of the open lifestyle, and from some men as well, is that I don't support my partners financially. I get that criticism because they are assuming that I'm in a polygynous situation where these women are all my live-in, sexually exclusive wives, but that's not the case. I don't believe in the theory that a man should automatically take care of a woman just because they're dating or whatever. That doesn't make any sense at all to me, even if we're married. Finances are determined on a case by case basis, and there is no one way to do it. I supported my wife financially for the first ten years of our marriage, and then we shared in the financial burden once we started our business together.

*SIDE NOTE: I know there are people out there who are simply haters of me and my lifestyle and look for any reason to trash it. I've had men do that and be like, "Well, Rakhem isn't even giving these women money." Some of these same men have tried to talk to my women and run that same line on them. They're just trying to get the pussy by any means necessary. What these men don't understand is by trashing me, it only makes my women want me more and them less. The more my name is in your mouth, the higher my stock rises. But hey, everyone can't be up on game.*

All that said, yes, I've helped out partners with bills and will continue to do so on a case-by-case basis. I have no problems sharing and supporting my partners in any way they need, and I expect the same from them. I have no issues paying for dates and trips and have done so on many occasions. I also don't have a problem with women paying for shit either. I actually really appreciate it when they do, especially when they have the means. I enjoy being taken out, treated well, and spoiled just like anyone else. I've had women pay for flights, hotels, trips, dates, bills, clothes, and the list goes on. I've had women offer to buy me condos and cars as well. I'm cool accepting any gift as long as I don't feel there's anything attached to it, like me giving you extra time or me dissing my other girlfriends.

What about my partners' boyfriends and husbands? Do they like me or hate me? It all depends. To tell the truth, not all my partner's husbands even know about me. Yep, that's right, and I don't have any problem with it. If you and your wife don't have the kind of relationship where you can share intimate information, then you don't have a right to know, and she doesn't have the right to know who you're fucking on the side. Another way to say it is that some of my partners are in monogamous marriages, which means they can't tell their spouse the truth about their lives. To me, that's just a part of monogamous marriage where they can't tell each other the truth about how they really feel or what they really want. Monogamous people would never admit it, but it's true in ninety percent of the cases. First of all, the "admitted" infidelity rate is above sixty percent. That's proof that most monogamous people aren't telling each other the truth. We shouldn't have to look further than that for the truth of what monogamous marriage actually is versus what it claims to be. Like I always say, "Monogamous marriage is built on a lie at its very foundation." Anyway, dating a married woman who's lying to her husband is standard practice in those relationships, and I'm not here to judge anyone's marriage. What she does or doesn't share with her husband is not any of my business. I'm dating her, not him. So those men aren't mad at me because they don't know about me. I guess you could say we're not friends either. I haven't fucked a woman married to a friend or associate of mine and prefer to never go there. When I say, I'll fuck a man's wife, in most cases, I don't know him personally, I make an assessment that he's fucking someone on the side, or I determine that his and his wife's relationship is pretty much over when it comes to closeness and intimacy. I just make my own personal assessment. If I feel he loves her, is being true to her, and is a solid individual, then I'll often pass on that situation. But if I can tell he's a player, whether it's through my own personal assessment or information his wife is giving me, then it's game on. Welcome to the Player's Ball brother. Don't hate the player, hate the game. What you put out, comes back to you strong. It's just the rules of the game.

And for those who are wondering, yes, I'm aware of and cool with any potential consequences that come with fucking another man's wife or woman. But it's not even about that for me because it's up to the man as to whether he's going to claim ownership over a particular woman. Meaning, he doesn't have to be married to her or even dating her to claim she's his and to take out his frustrations on any man courting her. I learned this lesson the hard way in high school when my girlfriend's ex-boyfriend, jumped me behind the school after a nighttime basketball game because he was mad or jealous of his woman moving on from him. He hit me with two fists full of rolled up quarters and knocked me the fuck out. My face was fucked up too. That was my introduction to the game. It's up to the man whether or not the new guy is violating or not. In other words, it's the wild, wild west out in this motherfucker. So, yes, I'm clear on the danger and all relevant risk factors.

I've had men do preemptive strikes by trying to befriend me or get coaching from me as an attempt to keep me away from their wife or girlfriend. That doesn't work if that's the intention. Meaning, if you're just hitting me up to keep me away from her, then I'll see it clearly and ignore the attempt. This will happen because the wife will mention my name or that she's attracted to me, causing the husband to force a "bro-code" protocol on me, but I always see through it. Again, the game is old, and I've been in it for a while.

In general, men don't like me because I encourage the concept of freedom in marriage, and they don't want their wives fucking anyone except for them. I get it because none of us really wants that in our hearts. It takes maturity and development to really want the best for your wife, even if you're not included in it. That said, I do date a number of women who are in an open marriage, and those men are usually cool with me - at least on the outside. I've had some good relationships with my partner's husbands, and I've had some that are fucked up like the one I will talk about later in the book with Isis. My view is it's really none of their business what their wife and I do. If they don't trust their wife, they should get a new one that they do trust, but I'm not here to make you feel better about your union. That's up to you and her.

I kind of think husbands should be thanking me because I'm

giving your wife what she needs and desires. It's keeping her from having an attitude around you, or even worse, ripping your head off. I'm helping to chill out her emotional interactions with towards you, and for that, I should be appreciated. It's just my thoughts on the matter. I mean, if I'm sending her home happy and relaxed, that helps your marriage. She'll be willing to support and treat you better. I know it's a harsh reality to accept, but it's the truth of the matter.

Are there any cases where my partners would like to marry me in a legal sense? Absolutely there are. I've had numerous partners desire it. Some talked to me about it. Others never said anything because they didn't think it was actually possible partly because I've always said that I would never divorce Kenya. So, let's talk about those two topics: (a) marrying other partners and (b) whether Kenya or I would ever divorce. First of all, let me say that the reason I'm open is that I withhold the right to move in any direction in my life without the concept of violating some oath, rule, or agreement. So, the concept that I'm locked into my marriage with Kenya or that I'm locked out of marriage with other partners is false. I can do what I want, just like Kenya can do what she wants. If she wanted to divorce me and marry another partner, that's her prerogative. What can I say other than things change, and that's one of the few constants we're aware of in our universe. So, is it possible that Kenya and I could divorce because one or both of us wanted it? Sure. It's just that we have no plans on divorcing at this time, and we haven't really seen a need to bring that option on the table. That said, I'm open to marrying another partner post-divorce with Kenya or in a spiritual sense. I'm fine having women in my life who are actual wives because of what they represent in my life, life partners who play a critical role in my mission and work. That said, I would question the reason why I would need to get legally married to anyone if Kenya and I did divorce. What's the actual reason and benefit to me of getting married again? At this point in my life, I don't see any benefits outside of creating a legal bond to help combine the assets we both own. Meaning, if I were to be with a woman who wanted to share her wealth with me and she wanted to protect my interest in that wealth, then I can definitely see that as a reason to get married. It would have to be a contract based reason for the marriage. I don't need marriage for love or commitment. Actually I see the contract of marriage as something that gets in the way of love. Love and contracts don't mix in my mind. But in short, I'm open to it. Each scenario would have to be evaluated on its own. I refuse to make any blanket statements about what I may or may not do with my life or relationships.

What about when my partners desire to get married to someone else? Wouldn't I feel possessive or insecure about them moving on to a more permanent relationship scenario like marriage; especially, if it means that we can't be together anymore? One thing about open relating is that you understand relationships are transitional. You realize that people change, and so do their needs. Nothing is meant to stay the same forever. If any of my partners decided to end our relationship and get legally married to someone else, I'd be happy for them. Why wouldn't I be when I'm married? I want everyone to have what they want when it's possible. Just because it may be uncomfortable for me doesn't mean I can't support it or be happy for the bigger picture. I know I can't give my partners long-term, exclusive, committed partnership, so I encourage them to find it if that's what they want. Sure I would be sad about it, but that comes with the territory. We're going to experience these emotions throughout all of our relationships.

That brings the conversation to holidays, vacations, and special days. Right now, Kenya and I reserve Thanksgiving and Christmas as a time to visit our extended families. We might go to visit her family on Thanksgiving and then my family for Christmas. Part of this is for our children to be able to see cousins, aunts, uncles, and grandparents. We have had a few scenarios in the past where we spent these holidays with other partners, but those were rare cases and didn't really work out that well. The families ended up rebelling at the break in tradition, and it turned out to be more trouble than it was worth. For example, I went to spend Thanksgiving with Southern Bella one year when she and I were dating more seriously. Kenya's family gave her a hard time about it. I had a great time with Southern Bella's family, though. Either way, that would be the last time we tried something like that because I didn't want Kenya to be subject to that kind of abuse from her side of the family. They could be exceptionally verbally abusive at times, and they were already against our open marriage in the first place.

In terms of what my wife or partners are "allowed" to do, my philosophy is their life is their life. They can choose to date or fuck whomever they want, and it's really none of my business. In reality, I'm not for the "allowing" concept because adult humans in a "free" society can do what they want. I don't own my women; therefore, I don't dictate their movements or choices, just like they don't dictate mine.

I should take the time now to discuss one of the struggles that I (and I'm sure others) have in the open relating world. It's the need to battle my monogamous tendencies. Meaning, having been raised in monogamous culture, I still have leanings towards things like hierarchy, specialness, and the desire to prioritize partners that show more sexual exclusiveness towards me.

Actually, I've had partners who've tried to separate themselves from others by being sexually exclusive with me. They will be quick to point out their dedication to me and our relationship. This indirectly highlights how my other girlfriends can't necessarily be there for me in the same way because they are distracted with other partners. We see this in the monogamous culture where "historic dedication" ("saving" themselves for or having few sexually encounters before marriage) is used to gain higher favor with their eventual spouse. In the dating world, it's referred to as keeping a low body count to increase your status as a potential spouse, and it's usually, but not exclusively, applied to women. My job is to ignore that narrative as a barometer of my partners, and instead, to look only at our chemistry and connection to determine what we'll be together. In terms of ranking partners or hierarchy, I really only look at our connection and what each partner is providing in my life as a determinant for what role they play in my life. Other factors might play into it like sexual chemistry and attraction as well.

So there's no ranking of girlfriends, and to that point, there are no titles that signify rank for me. All of the women I'm dating (meaning we have an understanding to be together in some capacity, we love one another, and we connect sexually) are girlfriends or partners to me. There's really no difference between those terms. If I know I'm going to be with a girlfriend for life, then I might call her a life partner. If she's genuinely a true one-hundred percent rider for me and my mission, then she's the equivalent to a wife. I would have no problem referring to her as such because that's what a wife is to me - a life partner who's a rider without any questions, hang-ups, or hesitations. That said, a life partner doesn't pull rank over a partner in terms of time or specialness. A wife, on the other hand, would be someone I would probably spend more time with just because of the role she's playing in my life. Meaning, the simple fact that she's choosing to show up for me in a certain way is what is going to afford her more time with me and most likely command more of my energy. For me, it's just mathematics instead of ranking. The bigger the role you play in my life, the more time we'll spend together. Riders are usually the ones who are playing the biggest roles, which is why they're referred to as riders. It's pretty straight forward.

I should take the time to talk about the title debacle. Historically, this has been a sore spot in my open relating life. Titles (i.e., wife, life partner, girlfriend, etc.) have been so important to some of the women I've dated throughout the years. I've had women who've really wanted the title of "wife" even though they realized we weren't going to be legally married. Also, there were women outside of my relationships who were critiquing me. Many of them had the same mindset where they felt I should give certain girlfriends elevated titles as a way to solidify their importance in my life. I'm not going to sit here and say that I don't get why these women were looking for titles, but it wasn't then and isn't now a priority for me. I've had women break up with me because I wouldn't give them the title they wanted and not speak to me to this day because of it. I've had women look at other girlfriends and say they deserve a title that elevates them above the other girlfriends because their importance is greater. Other women were careful to try and not offend Kenya and her position in my life by not assuming the title of wife. That's where the life partner title actually came from. It was like, how can we symbolize your importance in my life without actually calling you a wife? The solution was a life partner. It wasn't even something that I read about somewhere, but something we naturally came up with to accommodate the needs that were being presented at the time. It was after shit really hit the fan that I had to do away with special titles all together and just use girlfriend.

Over time, I started to use the word "partner." In some cases, I would use "life partner," but I definitely had to take a break from doing anything that might imply specialness or rank. At the same time, I had to make public declarations that there would be no ranking of partners and that everyone was equal; however, not the same. This simply created a different set of issues because "equal" means "the same" to a lot of people. This opened the door for time comparisons, which obviously will never be the same. I don't even want them to be the same because every relationship is different. At the end of the day, I had to realize that my girlfriends' desire for a special title had to do with their insecurity about our relationship and their future with me. This means I needed to do a better job of reassuring my girlfriends that we were solid and that we would build something based on our unique connection.

Long-distance relationships? The social media age has made connecting with women from anywhere in the world so incredibly easy. Most of my girlfriends have come from social media connections, which means most of my girlfriends have been long distance over the years. To be honest, I'm really not into long-distance relationships because the communication requirement is so high. So, I simply let my partners know that I won't be communicating very much. I just can't do it. I've done it, and it's way too consuming for me. It's like the long-distance relationships with intense communication were taking up more time than the local ones. Then you have the phenomena of video calls, which is even more restrictive. Back in the day, I could just talk on the phone with the headset on and the phone in my pocket and still get shit done. But now, these younger women want to video call, which means I have to hold the phone up with one hand and look at the screen half the time. It's a mess. No thanks. We'll check in here and there. Just know that I love you and want to see you and that our lack of talking is not an indication of a lack desire to want to see you.

I realize that it takes time to build intimacy between people, and sometimes that requires talking and texting frequently in the beginning. I'm all for that. I also know that a level of contact should be maintained so that people stay connected. I'm down with the "Grand Rising" first thing in the morning, "Thinking about you," "Missing you," and "Good night" texts. And I always tell my girlfriends to reach out to me whenever their heart desires it but to please be patient and understand that I may not text back right away. Speaking of which, I'm so happy to be out of that paradigm where not texting someone back was a cause for a fight or an argument. I hated those days where a girlfriend would be like, "I texted you over an hour ago, and you didn't respond." Now all my partners know to not expect an immediate response from me. I could be with another girlfriend, or writing, or sleeping, or not paying attention to my phone, or just not feeling like talking right now, and that has to be ok. The open relating lifestyle allows all of us to get what we need from wherever we can find it. That means that if you really need to talk about your day, feel free to find a partner who's available and open to that whenever I'm not available. It might actually be more of a primary type partner like your husband who's there with you every day or someone else who is really into talking and texting. That way, we don't expect one person to deliver everything we need and want in a relationship. It just works much better for me.

Other than that, I'm fine with long-distance relating even though I'm not really into traveling. Going through TSA sucks, and sitting on a plane for four hours sucks too! I've done enough flying to last me for this lifetime. I mean, I'll still do it, but I'm not eager to jump on a plane or drive for five hours. At this stage in my life, I really appreciate my local girlfriends and love to focus on them as best I can. Interestingly, I am writing this section as I sit on a plane flying from San Francisco back to Asheville, North Carolina.

The long-distance discussion leads right into the question of having the time to date as many women as I do. Again, the best thing about open relating is the ability to be really authentic with myself and with my partners about what I want. So, I'm really only engaging with women in ways that are comfortable for me. Communication is a prime example of what I'm talking about. When people think of traditional relating, they think of being on the phone with someone all day every day, but that's not what I enjoy. I'd rather talk here and there, and focus the majority of my time on whoever is in front of me or just be by myself. So that right there saves me a ton of time because there's no requirement to spend a bunch of time with someone unless we are physically together. The main reason for this is because I love to be by myself. I often describe myself as a recluse. My mother gets angry with me when I say that because I'm so great in social settings, which is true, but I prefer being by myself. My theory is that introverts are the best at social interaction because they desire to be as effective and efficient at it as possible so they can get through it unscathed and get back to being by themselves. It's just a theory. But to honor my mom's wishes, I'll just settle for the introvert label.

So, I spend most of my time by myself, and all my girlfriends know I'm like that and really don't bother me too much about it. Yes, they want to see me, but they get how I am. My girlfriends also know that I have a lot of other girlfriends and that my time is limited. Again, they don't love it that I'm seeing so many other women. Still, they get it, so it helps them manage their communication with me and their expectations of seeing me. Additionally, they know I'm an entrepreneur and business person and have needs there, not to mention my family at home. The long and short of it is, I have time. I actually have more time dating a ton of women inside an open relating structure than I did dating just one woman inside of a monogamous structure. Again, it only makes sense when you refrain from applying monogamous principles to open relating. I can't be everything to everybody, so I don't even try. That frees me up to live my life and connect with my partners naturally and organically.

Another question I get is, "Why not just be single if I'm going to date so many women?" If you're monogamous, then this question makes sense because those people only see one way to relate. In a monogamous culture, there is literally only one box to fit into. Anything outside of that box is for single people. But in open relating, we can all create our own ways of relating and write our own rules. So, for example, if I know that I'm going to be with one of my girlfriends for life and that we're going to build something together where the institution of marriage would support it, then I would consider marriage. When I look at my relationship with Kenya, we have a collective mission to raise our children and expand the consciousness of the planet, so it makes sense for us to do that work inside of a marriage. We also don't plan on ever separating or divorcing, so marriage is a great institution to support our union. Obviously, marriage doesn't mean sexual exclusivity for us, so our open relating lifestyle doesn't violate our marriage vows. It's not that I plan for any of my relationships to end. It is assumed that none of my relationships will be of the same quality and intensity. We're all not building an empire together or family or a business or whatever. Some of my relationships are just free and easy, and we're going with the flow for as long as the connection and desire are there. We're choosing not to burden our relationship with plans, expectations, or formalities. Other relationships do carry those formalities, which is why they may carry a more formalized structure to them.

In a monogamous culture, marriage is often tied to a type of morality or goodness, which makes open relating wrong for them or anyone engaged in that kind of thinking. I know most people think that morality is a standard thing that most people agree on, but I don't. Morality is simply a set of beliefs that a person subscribes to that they label as better or higher than all other beliefs. So if open relating is immoral to you, that's simply your belief. I subscribe to a different set of ethics and moral thinking; therefore, there is nothing immoral about open relating or living life on your terms. That can bring us to the religious discussion too where people will choose and practice a religion that matches their level of desired morality. If one believes in sexual fidelity as a part of their moral code, chances are they've found (or chosen to interpret) a religion to match that morality making open relating a sin. Again, that's their belief, not mine. Open relating matches up with my spiritual beliefs perfectly, so in my mind, I'm in alignment.

My definition of marriage is an arrangement where two or more people agree to love and support one another and grow together to the best of their abilities for the duration of that arrangement. That's it. Marriage, in my book, doesn't have anything to do with religion as all evidence points to marriage existing before religion. It doesn't have anything to do with sexual exclusivity either because the evidence points to marriage also including plural relationships and not being tied to sex until recently. For example, polygyny is just as old as monogamy and is still practiced today.

Another good discussion is whether I've hurt women whom I've dated because they really wanted a family and sexual exclusivity with me. Are they using our open relationship as a vehicle to ultimately reach that goal, or are they simply naive in their belief that they can actually be open and happy at the same time? Another similar question is whether only women of low self-esteem would engage in a practice where they are sharing a man rather than having a man to themselves. These are fair questions. First of all, I have hurt women I've dated since being open. Some of them wanted more from me than I was able or willing to give, and they left the relationship hurt or disappointed. In some cases, I've made promises or commitments that I've failed to keep, which again resulted in real hurt. Indeed, there have been women who've wanted to be in a family with me and some who've wanted children. Some were fine being a second wife, while others wanted something separate and apart from what I shared with Kenya. A few times, I believed I felt the same way only to change my mind later or see that it just wasn't practical for where I was in my life at that time.

I understand now that the hurt I inflicted was caused in part by my inexperience in functioning inside of an open marriage, and in part, simply by a character issue on my part where I lacked integrity. Either way, I definitely take responsibility for my failings and learnings along the way. That said, these issues are not really any different from when I was in sexually exclusive relationships. My character (or lack thereof) and lack of relationship experience contributed greatly to the demise of those situations as well. In other words, my honest assessment is that I've done equal damage regardless of the relationship structure. I believe this to be the case for all people. I don't believe any relationship structure can shield us from character or a lack of experience actually relating to other human beings. For example, there are many men in monogamous marriages who have dating profiles saying they are polyamorous. These men cheat on their wives and deceive other women not because they are monogamous, but because they lack integrity. I could blame the monogamous culture for their behavior because it is common in monogamy. In reality, it always reverts back to one's quality of character.

I also don't see women (or men) who openly relate as having low self-esteem. Self-esteem issues exist across classes of people and regardless of the relationship structure one practices. A common narrative in monogamous culture is that women who openly relate are desperate to have a man under any circumstances. That they're willing to have a piece of a man rather than a whole man to themselves because they don't believe they deserve more or better. I don't subscribe to this belief. I think everyone is doing the best they can in the relationship world and trying to figure things out as they go. People sometimes find themselves willing to try something new because they didn't find the success they desired in whatever they were doing before. It's not always about lacking confidence in oneself. That said, the low self-esteem argument can be made with women in monogamy as well. Some women may seek monogamy because they are fearful of being alone or judged by family or friends about being older and single. Some women are described as "having settled" because they married a man, or stayed in a marriage, not out of happiness, but because they didn't think they could do much better due to their lack of self-worth or confidence. So the argument can go both ways, which is why I don't see open relating as a symptom of having low self-esteem.

Another big question is whether open relating is just about sex. No relationship, in my opinion, can be just about sex because I believe you have to actually feel something for someone to engage sexually with them. I know my stance contradicts what most people believe. They can point to so many examples of where relationships or sexual encounters apparently lacked love and consideration or were even cruel. There are situations where sex was simply taken without consent. I get all of that, so I'll leave each person to maintain their beliefs. That said, just because I steal something from someone doesn't mean I don't love them or care about them. Sometimes we determine our needs in the moment are more important than someone else's and are willing to hurt them in the process. It happens all the time. Actually, I would say most of the hurtful things we see in the world happen between "loved ones," where the ones we thought cared about us the most seemed to cause us the most hurt and pain.

But the philosophical discourse isn't really the point here. I personally can't connect with a woman sexually unless I love her. I've also never had a purely sexual relationship. I don't even know what that is. Yes, I've had relationships that were highly sexual and others where most of our time together was spent having sex, but that doesn't mean there was no love there because there always was, without exception. That said, there's nothing wrong with sex, so even relationships that are dominated by sexual activity between two consenting adults should never be a problem. So what if two people decide to have sex three times a day, every day for the rest of their lives? Or what if someone decided to have twenty sexual partners and never become exclusive or build a family together or whatever? What if all we choose to do is have sex and rarely go out to eat or talk politics? Again, consenting adults should have the freedom to express themselves in the way they'd like, even if it goes against your idea of morality. I've never bought into the "sex is a sin" narrative that religion so often espouses. Also, props to those couples who find their sexual connection so compelling and fulfilling that they want to have sex all the time. I see that as a blessing; especially, considering all the sexless marriages out there and all the absolutely terrible sex happening out there.

Speaking of sex, I believe sex is critical to maintaining a healthy mental and emotional outlook on life as well as the way to stay intimately bonded to our partners. At this stage of my life, a solid sexual connection with any partner I'm with is mandatory. The sex has to be amazing and energizing in order for me to stay in the relationship. There's no better way for me to get close to someone I love than to literally be inside and intertwined with them. And let's be clear - when I say sex, I mean, raw, ejaculatory sex without barriers. I mean, skin on skin, hard penis inside wet pussy kind of sex. Anything else is a lesser version of sex for me and I try not to indulge in anything that takes away from the full experience. For a big part of my sexual life, I was a dedicated condom wearer, mostly because I was scared of getting a woman pregnant. When I look back on those days, I can see where I wasn't "fed" and energized by sex in the same way I am now. I was basically masturbating inside of a woman instead of actually feeling her and connecting with her. The act itself left me depleted and tired; whereas, now I'm energized. Instead of wanting to go to sleep after sex, I'm up and excited, and my mind is racing. It has also helped me become more deeply bonded with my partners and be able to feel them more intensely. Not just the feeling of their body and wet pussy, but their emotions as well. It's just an overall closer experience for me. The open relating lifestyle has allowed me to speak about my truth when it comes to sex in terms of what I want and what feels good to me. It's given me the freedom to communicate better with my girlfriends during sex and be more open to hearing them as well. If a potential partner and I don't agree on how to engage in sex, we simply agree to not move forward and maintain a platonic relationship. It's been such a gift to not feel like I have to force a relationship with anyone and simply allow myself to connect with women who are in alignment with me. I never have to feel like I'm going to lose out on an opportunity because I know I'll find other women in the world who will be more aligned with my wants and needs. I can just let it happen.

In terms of how I choose partners, I tend to let them pick me first. I like it when women give me a sign that they're interested in exploring a relationship or sex with me. It doesn't mean that women have to come up and talk to me, but I generally need to see a sign of her interest, like a stare or her jumping in my inbox or whatever, before I pursue her. I've had my experience of choosing and chasing women before, and it's not fruitful. It also opens you up to mistreatment because the woman is usually indifferent to you and the relationship, especially when things get challenging. If I'm the chooser and pursuer, it sets me up to do most of the work and be the primary stakeholder; meaning, the only one with something to lose if it doesn't work out. If she chooses me and I pursue her, we create a balance from the start as two people who put in equally to get things started. I like the mutually vested interest and action to match it. It also allows me to set the terms and conditions of our interaction. I can be honest and upfront about what I want and what I can and can't do in the relationship. If I'm both the chooser and pursuer, I'll have a tendency to hide some of my needs and desires to appear more appealing to the woman I'm pursuing. This starts the relationship out on rocky ground. It incorporates a lack of communication and authenticity from the beginning, which will be hard to reverse later on. In addition to all of that, when a woman chooses me, the passion is so much stronger and intense in the relationship, and when it comes to sex as well. There's nothing like someone who really wants to be with you versus someone who is lukewarm on their attraction to you. It's like, what's the point of being in a relationship with someone if there's no passion? I'm not saying it has to be super crazy, but it needs to be something. There's got to be some want and desire there for me to be fully engaged. If a woman chooses me and I'm not interested in pursuing a relationship, then I just let her know, and nothing happens past that point. Again, it has to be mutual and equal for me to engage in it.

What about breakups? Well, I believe that we never really break up with anyone once we choose one another, but that relationships change and transition all the time. I believe that energy underlies all relationships, and it is fueled and sourced by our desires for one another. Those desires will wax and wane over time and be the primary drivers for how much time we spend together and our level of communication. When the energy is high, we will both naturally gravitate towards one another. When it wanes, we'll naturally separate from each other. The only things that get in the way of the energetic flow of a relationship are our judgments (i.e., thoughts) and our physical proximity to one another. Sometimes I feel like I should be talking to someone more than I am even though the energy isn't pulling us to naturally do that. As a result, I'll sometimes find myself forcing the issue, which doesn't feel good to me at all. Other times, I may be close in proximity to someone, but don't really have the energy (i.e., desire) to see them or be with them. I've had this happen to me a few times when I've had women move close to me only to see the energy between us go through that waxing and waning cycle. It's created problems in the relationship because feelings of fear and insecurity on their end and guilt and shame on my end arise, further hampering our ability to be objective. Other times, I find myself far away from a partner, but with an overwhelming desire (i.e., energy) to see them. This creates a judgment (thought) to make plans to live closer together based on how we both feel about one another at the time. But when the energy between us begins to wane again, guilt can come up for not wanting to go through with previous plans of living together. The cycle just continues from there.

The result for me is to just be fluid in my relationships and allow myself to ride the waves without feeling shame. I try not to force anything while simultaneously honoring how I feel. If I want to talk to one of my girlfriends, I just call them without taking it personally if they don't answer or don't feel like talking at that time. If I want to see one of my girlfriends, I make plans to see them. If not, then I don't, even if we had plans set up already. I know that can be frustrating at times, but it's honest. All of my girlfriends learn over time how I move when it comes to the flow of energy in the relationship and make the adjustment accordingly. I flow the same way when it comes to sex. If my body is saying no then I try to honor it and when it says yes, I try to do the same. Again, this can lead to fear and hurt feelings on both sides sometimes, but it's honest. What helps is when I have conversations with my girlfriends about my feelings and explain it's just the way my body and energy work, and it's nothing to take personally. This philosophy has been the best way for me to find peace and happiness in my life in general. Accepting the highs and lows, the waxing and waning, and being fine with those cycles knowing they are a constant in almost all areas of life.

Why I don't identify as polyamorous, even though I am? It's too confusing because of all the flavors of polyamory that exist out there. There are so many ways to do polyamory and so many types of poly that I find myself having to explain myself after already explaining myself. Not only that, but each of my partnerships is different and they will have their own label and definition based on the official rules of polyamory. For example, some of my relationships are Don't Ask, Don't Tell, while others are Full Disclosure. Some of my partners are married and monogamous while others are polyamorous and single. Some of my relationships are private while others are public. I have some partners that no one knows about and others that everyone knows about. How I function in each of these situations is different based on the relationship itself. So there isn't any single term other than Open that can describe my relationship lifestyle. I'm Open to whatever I feel I want to do today. That could stay the same forever or change tomorrow. For me, Open describes me living my authentic life whatever that may be. The entire point of moving away from monogamy is to escape monogamous culture which is heavy on labels and definitions and the corresponding judgments that come with that. Unfortunately, we've seen the same judgmental tendencies carry over into the polyamorous community as well, and I feel it's a waste. The goal is freedom without judgment, not a new set of rules and categories for judging people.

When I say that each relationship is specific unto itself, I think it's best summarized in a quote I read online. A man approached a woman and asked her if she was single. Her response was, "I'll decide after we get to know each other better." This is the reality of relationships for me. This is why infidelity is so high in monogamous marriages. People fail to realize that the label you give yourself isn't at the top of the hierarchy in determining love, romance, and human connection. What comes first is our innate desire in combination with other people regardless of anything we define ourselves as or our nationality or race or gender or whatever. Love and connection don't care about your rules, labels, and definitions. It's going to do what it's going to do, So, the most intelligent thing we can do is to operate within a relationship framework that allows for pretty much anything to happen. That is what Open is. It's the box without walls that allows totally and completely authentic expression regardless of what that expression is. Does polyamory allow for one-hundred percent authentic expression? No, it doesn't; thus, my resistance to putting myself into a box that continues to limit the human experience.

# ~ 3 ~

**PART 3: Trials, Tribulations, & Lessons Learned**

I'VE DATED SCORES OF women throughout my almost fifteen years of open relating, and what I learned most was who the fuck I am and what the fuck I want. That's what the entire journey has been about for me - finding myself.

My relationships have been everything from beautiful diamonds to complete shit shows and everything in between. But from that perspective, they've all been beautiful. PART 3 contains selected stories from my relationship journey that helped shape my philosophy illustrated in PART 2.

The Early Open Relating Years

There's definitely a big difference between my earlier experiences with open relating versus my later years. I've also been able to make a lot of observations about myself, about love, as well as people's intentions, fears, and motivations. I can honestly say that my lack of experience at the beginning of my open relating journey contributed greatly to many of the challenges and relationship failures that I experienced.

The first thing I had to realize was that I was incredibly thirsty for sex, love, intimacy, new experience, and nurturing. In a monogamous culture, people usually just cheat to find love and break the monotony of their relationship, but I wasn't doing any of that. I was staying physically loyal to Kenya until we actually started our open relating journey. The result was that I needed some serious attention and connection from a woman. I needed hot sex on a platter and a change in scenery.

# Diamonds are Forever

I describe being in love as the feeling of being physically captivated, emotionally enthralled, and mentally consumed with someone else such that they become an addiction to you. The person triggers your passions such that you can't control yourself even if you wanted to. But you don't want to control yourself because the feeling is so surreal and overwhelming that you'd rather bask in involuntary, reflexive, abundant bliss rather than the mediocrity represented by your life to this point. It's intoxication, and it's no different than the draw we feel towards alcohol, sweets, drugs, or video games. It's the complete activation of our dopamine response receptors as triggered by another person.

In my lifetime, I've only experienced being in love with someone four times. I had the feeling for a time with my college sweetheart as my very first love experience. Next, I had it with Diamond. After Diamond, I had it with Jessie and then finally with Southern Bella. What's common to all of these experiences is the intensity of the feelings I had for these women and the extent to which I would go to be with them in any possible capacity I could. I have had some other "in love" experiences that were similar, but not quite as long-lasting. One was with Ama when I lived in NYC, and the other was with Isis.

I had known Diamond for years before we ever connected sexually, and I had always had a crush on her from the first time I met her. Her smile was so infectious that it instantly uplifted my mood. Her energy made my spirit happy. That's the only way I can describe it. Being around her gave my spirit a boost of light that allowed me to continue on with life. I looked forward to seeing her anywhere I could. When I would watch her move and work, I marveled at how soft her touch was. Seeing her hands glide across tables and workspaces was like watching poetry in motion. Her skin glowed and carried a bright, youthful energy. Her eyes literally sparkled. I could always see the moisture in her eyes just like she was on the verge of tears or had just finished crying with a smile on her face. I think the old-timers called it "The Devil beating his wife" when the sun would be out, but it would be raining at the same time.

My feelings for her were confusing. Still, I was always able to keep our relationship in perspective and never flirt with her or make suggestions of wanting to get together. As I mentioned before, I had no interest in cheating on Kenya. That said, the attraction remained. I was both happy and sad when she got married. It was great to see her happy and in a solid family relationship with a couple of children. She was able to be a stay-at-home mother and raise her children. It was beautiful to see. We would continue to be friends for years to come.

Once Kenya and I moved into open relating, I was able to approach Diamond about my feelings for her. I remember when I did it and how she reacted. We went out to eat, which wasn't a big deal for us because we were social like that for years. Typically, we'd just talk about business, her talents and dreams, and what was going on inside of our community. All super standard for us. This particular night, we had finished eating and were sitting in her car about to leave. I explained that my marriage was changing structure, and Kenya and I were moving into a new space. She was confused and bewildered by it, but I still told her how I felt about her. She seemed really nervous and embarrassed and wanted to leave. She said it was a lot and wanted to go home. On her way home, she called me and told me that she had the same feelings for me, but was really nervous about it. I was just glad to hear that she felt the same way as me. Sometimes you can go through life feeling love and attraction for someone, and when that feeling is never reciprocated, it can be devastating. This is doubly true if you're in love with someone, which I was with her.

What was interesting is that nothing much really changed

about our relationship except we started talking more on the phone and texting a lot more. We were basically in contact with each other all day every day. It was the most intense communication I had ever had in a relationship to that point. It would only be rivaled in my future relationship with Southern Bella. It was almost like a slow, courting process. Actually, it was the longest courting process that I had ever gone through in my life. I want to say it took us a year before we had sex. It was incredible how slow we were moving, but at the same time, not surprising considering our friendship and background of being tied up in a conservative religious culture. Part of the long courting process was her hesitancy to engage with me at all because of her nervousness around it. She just wasn't used to an arrangement like Kenya and I had. Also, she was going through her own marital challenges after learning that her husband had cheated on her. She was so devastated and hurt by that news that she never, ever recovered, even to this day. She still has vitriol for her husband, although they have made strides over the years to be cordial and effective co-parents. After finding out about her husband cheating, she went on her own little cheating spree with various men that she knew. She had totally checked out of her marriage but was torn about how to move forward and whether or not to get separated or divorced. They would eventually get separated and then a decade later, finalize their divorce. I was sad about it as I watched it unfold, but was more focused on my desire to be with her than what happened with them.

I risked everything just to talk to Diamond. I risked everything to see her even though we weren't sexually active. I would take as much time away from work as possible to find conference rooms or take extended lunch breaks just to be on the phone with her. I would do my work with her on the line, take other calls, talk to coworkers, go to the bathroom, you name it. Whenever I was in the same city as her, I would stay out all night with her only to be tired as hell at work the next day. You would think we were fucking, but we only explored basic levels of intimacy. Come to think of it, I'm not sure how I survived that time. I felt like my balls were about to explode because of how bad I wanted to get in that pussy. I guess it was my overall enjoyment of being around her that got me through my extreme sexual desire for her. I spent money too. I filled up gas tanks, paid for everything we did, and stretched the family budget beyond the breaking point. That's one of my first golden lessons when it came to open relating - money. I've dipped into family funds so many times that it's ridiculous. The bottom line is you can't really date without access to disposable income. It wasn't a lot with Diamond because we were both conscious of staying within realistic budgetary limits. We would also leverage whatever travel money I got from my job. So if I stayed in a hotel, she would stay with me. Sometimes I would end up getting a hotel that was super far away from my workplace just so I could be within a reasonable travel distance for her to get to me. She would be nervous that her husband or people she knew would see her out with me. Actually, nervous was the understatement. She was scared shitless. She was so worried about her image and brand that the last thing she wanted to be known as was a cheater even though her husband had already established himself as just that. She's the one who taught me how to creep and have a relationship on the down low. She would point out all the things that women would look at to see if their man was cheating on them. I learned so much. I can see why men get caught cheating so much when you have women who do this level of investigation. I learned how to delete texts, monitor spending, where to go and where not to go, what to say and what not to say. I didn't know it went that deep. I can't even remember half the stuff she taught me because I never adopted any of those habits. And yet, it helped me understand what was happening in the monogamous relationship world. The one thing I do remember is our passcode protocol to start messaging one another. In order to start a conversation, she wanted to verify it was me talking so she would give me part of a phrase, and I would have to complete it. She really wouldn't text me back unless I answered the question correctly. It was like those security questions used when you're resetting your password on one of your online accounts, except these were incomplete phrases that were a part of a time we shared together. It was pretty cool, but also a bit over the top.

Once we started fucking, all bets were off. The already extreme behavior we were displaying got even worse. We fucked everywhere - parks, restaurant parking lots, parking decks, construction sites, hotels, vans, finger fucked while driving, in the projects, side of the road, inside every vehicle we could find, you name it. Her sex drive was insatiable, and I'd be fucking for my life damn near. She could fuck for hours, and I'd be like, "It's morning, and I need to go to work." Her pussy was wide, deep, and wet too. She was like a super soaker in a rainforest. It took me forever to get head from her, though, but it was worth the fucking wait. The most beautiful and softest lips you could ever imagine combined with the softest touch on earth made for the perfect head. She was always nervous about giving me head because she related it to a more exclusive relationship structure, which brings us to the eventual downfall of our relationship. We were basically on a path to be together. Our idea was for her to join my family with Kenya. That's the thing - I wasn't in full open relating mode with her. We were in a more polygynous type of mindset. We even talked about having children and everything, although I was hesitant about that, as she was too. She was also looking for something a bit more exclusive, where I was dating only her and Kenya. I was actually down with that for a long time until things got a bit hectic in our relationship towards the end.

My hesitation with adding her to the family was that I thought it would be too much coordination, management, and potential drama. I mean, I think she and Kenya would have gotten along great, but I could see some possible power struggles happening down the line. Another issue was I felt that I would want to spend more time with her than Kenya, and that would throw off the balance of a joined family situation. I mean, I was in love with Diamond and wanted to spend all my time with her, and it felt like the best way to do that was to have something separate from my other family. I also thought that bringing responsibilities into the mix would just weigh everything down and make our relationship monotonous, which defeated the point. So, I was torn. But the biggest thing that gave me pause was her intensity in general. She was the type of person who liked to micromanage your movements and behavior. As I said, she was an expert at picking up on cheating and lying, which is great if you're trying to identify if your partner is cheating on you, but it is torturous when you're simply trying to relate to someone. It started to become overbearing and even felt smothering at times. The major sacrifices and risks I took on the job to talk to her turned into expectations. I was beginning to feel unappreciated for my efforts to see and talk to her. What resulted was me trying to take space from her here and there just to get a breather and, of course, she noticed it right away. We would have conversations about how things felt different. For example, I would talk to her every morning while she was in the car. If I cut our conversation short or missed a day, she would panic and ask me what was going on. I felt ashamed at the fact that I started so strongly and intensely with her, but was unable to maintain it after a few years. I felt like I lacked a character quality that allowed me to be consistent in a relationship. I felt like I let her down, but I also felt legitimately burned out.

The beginning of the end came for us when she determined that I took a trip to see another woman instead of using that time to see her. She felt as though I was no longer prioritizing our relationship, and she slowly started pulling back herself. We'd have conversations where she'd tell me how things didn't feel the same and how my behavior towards her had changed. I would tell her that I was still in love with her, but she didn't really accept that from me. She was an "actions speak louder than words" type of woman, and my actions weren't matching up to the level of intensity that we had shared for the previous two years. Those were some rough conversations because she was right in that my actions had changed, but she was wrong in thinking my feelings for her had changed. They hadn't. She was still the most beautiful woman in my life and I didn't want to be without her. I still wanted to create something permanent and lasting with her, but things were slipping away. I was depressed about it. On top of that, whenever I doubled and tripled my efforts to do better and show up more in our relationship, the worse I felt. It was like running up a hill with a sack of rocks on my shoulders. It just felt heavy. I thought we just needed to change the structure of our relationship. We talked about her moving closer to me, but she was hesitant to do that without something more formal with Kenya. She was also hesitant based on how my actions had changed with her and I totally got that. The truth is, I know I'm changeable. I know I need variety and to switch things up to keep from getting bored. I know that I need space for myself, sometimes at the expense of loved ones. I know that I run from heavy structure and responsibility when I feel it might be overwhelming and monotonous. I have no problem admitting to these character traits and I communicated many of them to her as well. But that's being in love - it can make things frightening as hell when it appears that things are changing. Sometimes all you can think about is the potential loss as opposed to the probability of potential gain resulting from a change.

We were so deeply in love that we continued to stay in contact and talk to each other for years to come. She would tell me about her other relationships, and she would listen to stories about mine as well. She would even end up talking and bonding with some of my partners, but we never would become sexual again. She was too worried about disease and valued intense focus too much to date a bunch of people at one time. I get it. We're all different and want things the way we want them.

Did I mention that we fucked, literally everywhere? Oh yeah, I did. Did I mention that her eyes were so incredibly beautiful? They were. Did I mention that I love her to this day? Well, I do. We still talk every now and then. She's such a sweetie. She's brilliant and uber-talented. I'm almost one-hundred percent sure we'll never rekindle what we once had, but there's zero doubt that what we shared was one of the most impactful relationships either one of us would ever have. Not only the intensity of it but the timing for both of us. I was at the beginning of my open relating journey, and she was at the beginning of trying to find herself apart from being a mother and wife. She was starting to find her own path in life and move towards what she wanted as opposed to what others said she should have.

# Other Significant Relationships

My relationship with Diamond spanned years, but I had other significant relationships while we were fizzling out towards the end. My first official open relating relationship was with Donna, who I describe as D-Train in my book, *Finding Male Sexuality: My Personal Journey in Awakening the Masculine Sexual Self.* I called her D-Train because she was stupid thick like a caboose; plus, she loved that name. She knew she was a brick house. It was interesting meeting her because she introduced me to the fact that there are many children who grow up in second or third families. Meaning, their father is a man who has a legal wife that's not their mom but still maintains the family as if it were his only one. This is common in monogamy where a man will have multiple families that the wife and others in the community don't know about. Of course, in real life, word eventually gets out about these additional families, but they often exist in almost virtual obscurity for decades. What was interesting about her story was how normal everything seemed to her and her mother. It was just the way it was, and as a result, she was open to alternative dating arrangements. She wanted a husband of her own and would eventually get that, but she didn't shy away from men she desired simply because they had other women. I really respected that about her. It just felt real and authentic to me. What was also impressive about her was her understanding of the "first wife" concept. She would frequently direct me to do things to ensure my relationship with Kenya at home was solid. It's like she got that there is a certain way you need to handle your wife when you're dating other women, whether the wife knows about them or not. It wasn't a fear thing like with Diamond, but merely wisdom based on her growing up in an alternative family structure.

It was cool that I met her on a cruise, and she happened to live in the Atlanta area, which is where Kenya and I were living at the time. We couldn't hook up on the cruise because neither one of us had our own rooms, but we got together soon thereafter. It was clear that she wanted to have a family with me, but to be honest, she was further ahead in the open relating game than I was. Her outlook on family and what she wanted was refined, whereas I was out in the dating world still trying to figure things out. I guess you can say it was a maturity difference where she was the more mature one. She carried herself that way as well. Very cool with grace and elegance, which was super sexy for a voluptuous woman. It's just super impressive to see people out here with advanced relating skills paired with open minds outside of any kind of label like open, poly, or mono. These are simply folks who are looking to build their lives as best they can without forcing themselves into a box.

We eventually split because she was ahead of me in maturity, but I appreciate everything she taught me. Next, I would start dating the Tantric Goddess. She was also open to a polygynous lifestyle where I had Kenya as a primary wife and her as kind of a secondary wife. She wanted a family with children and a man to be with her a large part of the time. The primary reason we broke up was that I moved from Atlanta, where we were both living at the time, to New York City. Kenya and I moved for our career and to expand our business, which we were successful at doing. The distance, though, was something the Tantric Goddess and I couldn't overcome, but we tried. She came to see me once, and I went to see her, but we both just needed more out of the relationship, so we amicably parted ways.

When I was in New York, I had a couple of relationships, but nothing that was too serious. My deepest relationship was with a cutie from Queens. I remember she was super funny and gave great head. Her pussy was tops too, but she was kinda all over the place, which isn't unusual for New Yorkers. It just seems like they're always in hustle-mode. We had great times together, though. Kenya ended up meeting a guy she was super into, and they would wind up spending a ton of time together, which kind of left me semi-alone and without consistent intimacy. I mean, Kenya and I slept in the same bed, but we never had sex or intimacy because we were sharing a twin size bed inside of a five-bedroom apartment. It was super tight in there. I learned you must have your own place or at least your own room if you're going to be successful at practicing open relating. That was especially true in New York, where space was at a premium. So, Kenya and her guy were hitting it off super strong, and I was without a steady partner. In retrospect, it created a feeling of loneliness for me, which was kind of confusing, seeing as I was in a massive city with millions of people. I mean, you could walk by thousands of people in one day and never say a word to anyone. That was so new to me, but I loved the energy of the city anyway. There was a constant buzz that's hard to explain that seems to feed you like super oxygen or something. I still love it to this day. But that loneliness set me up for one of my more significant relationships in my open relating lifestyle to date.

## In Love with Southern Bella

One day I got an inbox from Southern Bella simply saying, "Hi. I had a dream about you. Hope all is well." I really didn't know her at all, and when I glanced at her picture, I didn't recognize her. Later I found out she was in one of our online programs, and she was digging my lectures, voice, and perspective, and decided to reach out. I eventually got back to her a few days later, and we started texting regularly until one day, she said, "You can call me, you know." It's weird, but I had almost forgotten about talking on the phone because that's when messaging was super hot and new. But we would eventually start talking on the phone, and our connection was incredible. We'd talk on the phone for like eight hours per day. I'd be at the park or walking the streets just on the phone with her. I could feel her energy through the phone and her texts if that makes any sense. I could feel her whenever we were talking or texting, and it was intoxicating. I was deep in love with this woman. Part of the attraction I had for her was her voice. If I had to guess what a siren's voice sounded like or how it affected someone, I would say hers matched that. It was on the high side, but it had a smoothness about it that made it super sensual and sexy without her trying. This relationship would end up shaping so much of my outlook on open relating that it's hard to even quantify. I learned about what being in love means to one's self-control.

I wrote a short blog post about her voice and how it affected me once I realized it. It was quite the revelation for me, so I wanted to express it the best way I knew how - through writing. Here it goes…

## And She Sings

I realized something profound a few years ago regarding what I loved so intensely about one of my partners. I say profound because ever since my introduction to tantra and sexual alchemy I've been on a journey of redefining what sex is, what attraction is, and where my pleasure comes from as a man during sex. I've documented this journey and the details of my sexual experiences with women in my book, *Finding Male Sexuality: My Personal Journey in Awakening the Masculine Sexual Self.* Tantra helped me appreciate the subtle aspects of a woman's beauty. It helped me appreciate her gifts and see her as a gift in and of herself. I was able to get away from focusing solely on hips, ass, legs, and breasts and see something so much deeper in her.

Have you ever been with a lover and the lovemaking is transcendent? I mean unexplainably, this is my soulmate, twin flame, for life kind of transcendent? It's just amazing almost every time like theirs some kind of psychic or past life connection between you.

I'm so grateful that she's in my life, I'm not sure what I would have done though if I found out that she was married – how do people cope with their twin flames being married? I'm sure this sort of thing has happened before. Luckily I don't have to experience it.

She once told me, "We must have been lovers in numerous past lives." That may or may not be true, but I discovered something about her and us that elevated my consciousness. I discovered what about her penetrates my soul when we make love.

It's her voice.

Not her talking voice, but specifically, it's her voice when we make love. When we begin to reach the highest heights. When we make love she sings. It's angelic and precise and soothing and melodic.

Her voice is like poetry when we make love. She doesn't have to say words or speak the English language. Just the sound of her voice alone penetrates my soul. Her moans. How she calls my name. Everything. It's all music to my soul regardless of the sounds she makes. It breaks down my false male bravado and brings out my vulnerabilities. The illusions I've built are replaced with the essence of my eternal self. Her vibration breaks loose my rigidness and hardness and eliminates the stress and tension. The posture I take as a man to deflect the tough world around me comes crumbling down when she sings to me. The emotions I hide inside and tuck away in the name of alpha masculinity come forth uncontrollably.

And when I'm broken down to my essence, naked, and bare, her voice builds me back up – fortifies me. It's the healing I need as a man. It's the experience that only a woman can give a man – stripping him down and summoning his essence, kissing it, healing it, and making it strong again.

I believe this is one of the true benefits of love making for men. If you allow her, a woman can make it all better with her voice. She can help you remember your highest self. That there is a soft place to land and a way to extract the pain in the gentlest way.

The beautiful thing is this realization with her allowed me to recognize the voice in all women. I was able to receive their song and see it as the healing gift that it is. I believe all women have this ability and hope that men will choose to go deeper than the surface of her to truly benefit from her gifts. I hope that men will choose to honor her and do the work to bring out these gifts.

If she trusts you, loves you, and feels connected to you she will sing for you and it will be a song more beautiful than you've ever heard before. It will be transcendent and cosmic and bring you back to the source of all things."

Not too bad, huh? If that doesn't sound like a man in love, then I don't know what does.

I was still living in New York when I arranged my first trip to see Southern Bella. She lived down south and wasn't near any major airports, so I had to fly into Memphis and then drive five hours to get to her. She lived in this small house that could only be described as a tiny home before tiny homes became a thing. It was two rooms and a bathroom with a small front and back porch. It was super cool. It was raining the day I went to see her. It was a little confusing finding her house, but I figured it out. She was super anxious to see me and was pressing me with texts and calls like, "Where are you at?" The truth was, I wanted to sneak up on her, and I also needed to get myself together a bit. Like do a mouthwash thing and check the mirror, but whatever. I pulled up to her house, and she was waiting on the porch for me. She was wearing this tight, fitted skirt and a tank top. I was super attracted to her in person. She was about five feet two inches tall, with a tight but thick ass and beautiful eyes and lips. I also liked her hands and feet. Actually, I was super into her hands and feet, almost like a fetish or something. To me, she just had beautiful features, and I enjoyed watching her and looking at her. She waved me into the house. I left my bags in the car and rushed up to give her a passionate hug and kiss. We went straight inside to her bedroom and started fucking. She later told me that's the fastest she's ever fucked a man after seeing him physically for the first time. It was kind of quick. It took me about fifteen minutes to actually get my erect penis inside of her. She later told me she was scared shitless that it wasn't going to fit and that the entire trip would be for naught. Once I got inside of her, though, the sex was incredible and passionate. It was the first time I got to hear her sing.

We would fuck thirteen times that weekend. I remember sitting on her couch and her just holding my dick and looking at it. It was like she was studying it and she said, "You've got a beautiful penis." and gave it a kiss. I really appreciated hearing that from her, but I kind of wished she would have just started sucking that motherfucker. It was interesting that we didn't do any oral sex at all that weekend. We just fucked. Later I would find out that she wasn't really into oral sex. She didn't really want to receive it, and she was kind of stingy when it came to giving it. It didn't matter because I was the same way about giving it. I wasn't a huge eater of pussy at that stage of my open relating life, but that would change later down the line. I'm pretty sure we fucked missionary every time, and the sex was dope every single time. I really like finding that one position that works amazingly for both parties and being one-hundred percent cool with doing it that way every time. I think they call that the silver bullet. Overall it was an amazingly connected trip and well worth the journey. Like I said, we were in love and wanted to be together more consistently. But the "in love" thing kind of makes you lose your mind a bit.

At first, I tried to move my entire family - Kenya, my three children, and our two dogs - into a communal house with Southern Bella and her daughter. I wanted us to move to her southern city and state, which is over five hours away from the closest major city. In hindsight, it was a ridiculous notion, but when you're in love, it makes perfect sense. We went through the entire process of finding a house and everything. Kenya was basically like, "What the entire fuck are you thinking about Rakhem?!" She even got her family involved, and they were like, "What the entire fuck are you thinking about Rakhem?! The lifestyle itself is bad enough, but to move to the absolute boondocks?" They were all right, and the deal fell apart, causing major strife between Bella and me. She thought that Kenya was against our relationship and that I lacked the seriousness to build something with her. Those things may have been true, but the reality was that a move like that just wasn't practical.

The move debacle proved to have a major impact on our entire relationship. Bella would bring it up every now and again as proof of Kenya's evil intentions towards her. It wasn't even close to our biggest problem, though, which was me fucking other women.

This was the first time in my open relating experience where I was challenged to live my authentic truth. I wanted to be with Bella so badly, but we were super long distance, and there was no way I was going to stop dating other women while we were apart. But Bella was a Libra and believed in the fairytale relationship and the concept of specialness, which basically boils down to sexual exclusivity. She understood that I was open and married and dating other women when we met. However, she didn't comprehend how I could be completely and totally in love with her and still be dating others. I understood where she was coming from because if I was local to her, I probably wouldn't be dating other women. Well, at least, not as much as I was when her and I were apart. But we were apart, and I was going to pursue yoni at all costs. I still needed love, touch, and physical intimacy. But here was the problem - Bella and I talked so much on the phone and text that when I went ghost on her, it set off alarm bells. She would be like, "Where were you last night? I called and texted you a few times." I think she already knew that I was with someone else because she could feel it. Also, I'm a terrible liar because I don't want to have to lie. After all, that's why I'm open to begin with, but if I don't lie, then Bella is going to be super hurt by the fact that I was out with another woman. I couldn't stand to see her hurt. I couldn't stand to hear her cry on the phone. Being in love will do that where your partner's pain becomes your pain; especially, when you are the potential cause for that pain. So I would tell her I was out on a date, and she would say, "Why Rakhem? Why?" Then sob on the phone.

Honestly, I didn't even know what to say to her in these moments. I was so confused about what I wanted to do for me versus how my truth would make her feel. This relationship actually had me questioning whether I even wanted to be open. I was like, I just need to get down to live with her two weeks out of the month so that we could have adequate time together and just forget about connecting with other women. I would just focus on her and Kenya. But that didn't feel one-hundred percent right to me; it felt about eighty percent, though. The issue is that it just wasn't practical. She lived too far away, and she had a daughter that she was responsible for all by herself, which limited her ability to move. I felt stuck, but again, the idea of going back to any kind of sexual exclusivity didn't sit right with me either. It just wasn't in my blood, but I strongly considered it.

I actually battle this scenario throughout my open relating life where I would have a slight desire to be exclusive because that's all I had known for all my life. Not only that, but I also craved a simpler life than I had been living. At this point, Kenya and I had been in the public eye on television, radio, and the subject of numerous articles. There was a lot of pressure to show up a certain way when you're being looked at by the entire world. This made me crave the simple, southern life a bit where I could just be out of the public eye entirely and just do my writing in private. A life with Bella offered just that, which made things difficult for me as well. So, I had all these thoughts, on top of being in love with Bella, pulling at me while I'm living in the biggest city in the country trying to survive on a day to day basis. It was tough.

But it wasn't just Bella who was jealous. After it became clear that I was going to continue dating, Bella looked for ways to cope with the pain I was putting her through. She looked for an outlet, and she found it with a basketball player named Cefereth. The first thing I'd like to say is, "Fuck this motherfucker." Ok, let's continue. So, she started dating this guy because we were open, right? But for her to do it with a clear mind, she decided to separate from me for a time. We stopped our communication and had only minimal contact here and there. We were still together when she first started dating him, but then she took space soon after they made things official. Those were some of the most painful times of my open relating life, and believe me, I've had many of them. Have you ever felt like your heart, chest, and ribcage were caving into your spinal column? Or like a giant cyclops was squeezing your body in his hands, and it was just crushing you? Yeah, that's how I felt. I mean, she was actually fucking this dude. I was pissed like a motherfucker. I love all human beings, but I hated this motherfucker for real. I remember talking to Bella one night, and she was like, "Well, I have to go because Cefereth is on the way to get me."

The good thing about being on both sides of extreme jealousy is that it gives you great context about yourself and the relationship. You can't gain understanding when you're just on one side of the jealousy. You have to be on both sides. You have to be the trigger for someone else's jealousy and be the one triggered by someone else's actions. Then it's like, "Ok, now I get it. Now I know exactly how you were feeling when I was out dating other women." So, I needed that perspective even though

I died every day that entire summer. What made it even worse was that song was out talking about "I'm going to sleep with an NFL player..." Every time I heard that song, I wanted to stab that ninja. Every time I heard that song, I felt like I was dying on the inside. There was no escaping how I felt. There was nowhere to hide. The pain was crushing my heart completely, and there was nothing I could do about it, but feel it and be mad. Somehow, that experience of feeling extreme jealousy sobered me up about my relationship with Bella. At the same time, it also gave me a different perspective on open relating. I realized I needed to seek balance in all of my relationships and not allow my happiness to be controlled by any one person other than me. I learned what it's like to be so into someone else that you lose yourself in the process. I learned the "in love" lesson. I had literally put all my love and happiness into Bella. Yes, I was dating other women, but the emotional connection wasn't the same, partly because I didn't open myself to experience that with anyone else but her. I was so in love with her that you could say I lost myself in her, and that just wasn't a good thing. Even when she and I were together, my intense focus and attraction to her ended up causing dissension between us. It made everything she did so critically important and oversensitized me to her words and actions, and that would get us into petty arguments about small stuff. It removed my ability to be reasonable, and that adversely affected our relationship. But I totally understand the draw toward intensity and passion. It makes everything feel so much more alive, but it also creates a shitstorm at times, which makes the relationship unsustainable.

That would be the last time I would allow myself to fall in love in that same way. There was just no way I was going back to something so volatile, no matter how amazing the highs were. Bella and I would date on and off for years after that. We still remain in contact every now and then but haven't dated again because I know she wants that intensity and exclusive focus, which I can't give her. As tempting as it gets to be with her and feel her again, I just can't do it. I would have to kill a big part of myself to be with her again, and I'm not willing to do that going forward.

But this wasn't just about being in love as the source of the challenge in the relationship. It was also about dating someone who was subscribed to a mostly monogamous culture of relating. Bella's tolerance for open relating was rooted in the fact that I was already open when she met me. Therefore, she had to have a level of acceptance of it. Otherwise, she would have had zero tolerance for me dating or having any kind of closeness with another woman. As I mentioned before, I continue to choose women with a monogamish vibe because of my draw to intensity and specialness. But these are generally the things at the root of failing relationships because neither of them can be maintained. I'm not saying there aren't any couples who haven't maintained the passion for thirty plus years out there. I'm just saying, I haven't seen them. The "successful" marriages I've seen have the component of friendship and intimacy as their base - not passion. Even many of those marriages are chock full of infidelity and emotional abuse, but they managed to avoid the divorce decree.

It's also interesting that most of the women who were attracted to me and observed my relationship with Bella, wanted the same type of relationship. Almost all of them said Bella got the best of what I had to offer as a man, and they would want a similar relationship with me as proof that I was into them in the same way. They wanted the intensity and the declarations of love and even the messiness. I can kind of understand where they're coming from. I think what they meant was that they could see I was clearly in love with Bella. To me, that seemed to represent the fairytale soulmate or twin flame relationship they apparently wanted. They wanted it even though, in the end, it didn't work for Bella and me. They wanted me to be as deeply into them as I was into her. Like I said, I get it. My theory is that every woman wants her man to be in love with her because it increases the probability he'll do almost anything for her and minimizes the risk of him leaving her or cheating. It also guarantees that she is the center of his world and the apple of his eye, so yeah, I get it. On my side, it just wore me out emotionally. From the inside out, I was just exhausted by the end of our relationship. I needed to be able to breathe again and the focus on myself.

## Rakhem as the Center

My next two relationships differed from earlier ones in that I was at the center of them from my perspective. I say this because the women I would start to date after Bella seemed to really love me for me and not just for the fantasy of what we could be. The first woman I met was Angelina, and she was super in love with me and was happy just being with and around me. She was married with children, so I never had an issue with her questioning my marriage with Kenya. She was also open and actively dating other men, so she didn't have an issue with me being open either. She had a super high sex drive and loved to fuck and wanted to please me, and that was something new to me. In most of my relationships, I was the giver and worker, but with Angelina, I became the receiver. She was the beginning of my journey to receiving exactly what I wanted in a relationship. She was the type of woman I was looking for and represented one of my best experiences in my open relating journey.

At about the same time I met Angelina, I also met Anisah, who provided the same exact energy. She loved me for me and was willing to give to me as a demonstration of her love. She gave to me sexually and through her kindness and support. Between Anisah and Angelina, I had some of the best sexual experiences of my life. I also had some of the easiest relating that I've ever experienced too. I consider my relationships with them to be the true beginning of really experiencing the bounty and benefits of open relating. Being with two women who loved me for me, embraced open relationships, and who allowed themselves to give to me from that place of love. Both of them were married and with children, and neither of their husbands liked me or approved of their open relating lifestyle. And yes, both of them had numerous other partners that they engaged with besides me. I consider my time with them to represent the golden years of my open relating experience because the effort was minimal, the integration of our lives was seamless, and the sex was off the charts. Going forward, I would use these two relationships as the standard for new partnerships. As of the publication of this book, they represent my longest-standing relationships in my open relating journey.

Interestingly, I tried to be closer and more traditional with both Angelina and Anisah, but in both cases, it didn't work out. I think it's because they're both still very heavily vested in their primary relationships, and I was fine with that. I mean, I was kind of hoping to spend significant time with them and even live with them part-time, but it just wasn't to be. That was another lesson I had to learn on my open relating journey and a necessary three-hundred and sixty-degree view of things. When a woman is married, it means she's tied up and delusions of being with her full time or even a lot of time just aren't realistic. It is the same exact lesson many women had to learn about being with me as a married man. I just have a lot of obligations at home with my wife and children. I won't even begin to be free until all my children are out of the house, and after that, I can't really say to be honest because I'm not there yet.

I'd like to think I'll be more freed up, but we'll have to wait and see. I learned this lesson not only from Angelina and Anisah but also by observing Anita's relationship. She was dating a man who wanted to be with her full time, but she was married. Once her children graduated high school, she and her boyfriend were going to be together full time. Low and behold, it didn't work out that way. He ended up getting frustrated and distancing himself a bit from the relationship. That's one of the things that helped keep me sober about my relationship with Anita. I realized that realistically, I can't bank on anything big happening there. I can't make any plans or have any expectations of her because it's just not smart. Women need to look at me the same way. I have a wife, three children, and a number of girlfriends that I deal with. Although I feel my time will be freer after my youngest son graduates from high school, I really don't know for sure. For that reason, I don't make any commitments that I can't keep. No promises of me living with you or spending time or anything. The best I can do is promise that we can do some long term visits or maybe some extended living situations. I can't guarantee that I will ever be able to live with you.

It's just that I've seen so many people who are so optimistic about what can happen inside of these new relationships. The fact that the hormones are racing doesn't help much either. In the polyamorous community, they call it New Relationship Energy or NRE. The monogamous community calls it the honeymoon phase of relationships. Scientists call it the activation of the hormone oxytocin, which causes you to bond more closely with your mate through childbirth. Whatever you call it, just know that initial energy most likely won't last. The promises or commitments you made during that phase will be in jeopardy once that energy wears off. Just a word to the wise.

## Excellence Personified = Edrea

I would have really great relationship experiences going forward after finding both Angelina and Anisah. The quality of women I was attracting and choosing back was at an all-time high. Another high quality girlfriend I had was Edrea. She was my first ride or die girlfriend. Don't get me wrong, Kenya was and is ride-or-die, of course, but things were too complicated with Kenya because of all of the dynamics within our family. Angelina was a ride-or-die girlfriend too, but she wasn't in a position to really be there for me because she had a husband who was super restrictive and insecure and she had responsibilities with her children. With Edrea it was different because she didn't have other partners or children so she could really show up for me.

What made our relationship situation unique was the fact that she lived with Kenya and I for an extended period of time. Her being in the house allowed her to be there for me in ways my other partners just couldn't. In general I don't have one partner interact with another because all it really turns into is a shitshow. That's my experience and what I've observed from polygynous and monogamous situations. It's also partly my doing because I don't really feel like managing adults to where they can now get along. I'm sure if I did more to facilitate them coexisting, things could work much better. That said, women who are fucking the same man usually find a way to compare and contrast themselves against this one and that one. It's not even about a gender thing in my opinion. It's just that in our culture women are under the most pressure to get married and be the queen and they can't do that if they don't have the ring. They can't do that if there are other women in the picture vying for their position. And there's no reality where the women aren't vying for position at least not in these modern times. Women have been preprogrammed in our culture not to trust themselves, their man, any woman, or their man's friends. I just gave you supreme game even though it's a well known fact in player's circles. I just had to say it again. That said, I was able to trust Edrea to handle dealing with my other girlfriends. It kind of happened by accident, but when it did I didn't hesitate to trust her to be my main ride or die.

Edrea was living in the house when Kenya and I got into a fight over some dumbshit. I don't even remember what it was about to be honest, but it didn't really matter. Kenya loves to go the fuck off and create all kinds of dramatics. She loves the physical confrontation too. It is what it is. Her and I got into something and I just left the house to avoid things getting out of hand, but I just walked up the street. Well, I turn around and Kenya is right behind me and her arm is wound up. Next thing I know, she throws a glass at me and it hits me in the mouth drawing blood and making me kind of dizzy. It was the second time in my life when I've been hit by someone and either felt dizzy or been knocked out. The first time was when I got knocked out behind a highschool after a basketball game. I mentioned earlier that my girlfriend's ex-boyfriend jumped me because he was pissed that I was going deep up in her. Fuck him by the way. But this was the second time. The glass was one of those thick glasses with the thick and hard bottom like the old school Scotch glasses you see in the classic black and white movies of the 1950s. My tooth is still loose to this day from that shit. But yeah, I felt dizzy and I didn't know what else she was going to do. As soon as she threw the glass at me, she turned and headed back to the house, probably because she thought I might come after her. I admit that back in the day I may have wanted to chase her down, but I was over the whole violence in relationships thing. I was done fighting Kenya in any way shape or form, but especially physically. I made a pact with myself that if she ever attacked me or threatened me that I would just call the police, which is exactly what I did. Again, back in the day, I would have made a different choice. I may have chased her down. I may have pushed her against a wall or even choked her out. Those were always my responses to her instigating physical violence towards me. The truth is, we were both drawn to the dopamine rush so I'm not even blaming her for coming at me the way she did all those years. I tended to be someone who gravitated towards violence with men as well even though I could count my physical altercations with men on one hand. No blame, but I knew the only way to get out of that behavior was to not take matters into my own hands because there was nothing I could do with Kenya that could really dissuade her from coming at me the way she did. I was prone to violence, but I wasn't the type of man to actually hit a woman or punch her or whatever. Strictly wrestling, bearhug restraints, and choke outs if it got to that point, which it did once. I remember that time well because I thought I killed her to be honest, but not this time. I called the police and they arrived in about twenty minutes. When they got to the house I was sitting in the grass across the street in a small park near the house. I had to sit down because I felt dizzy. Looking back on it, I suffered a concussion and it lingered for about three days. I walked over to the police officer while his partner knocked on the door. I told him, "I'm the one that called you guys." He took my information and asked what happened. I broke everything down to him and then they went to talk to Kenya to get her story. The officer came out and said, "She corroborated everything you said. She didn't deny anything. At this point, we need to take her to the station. Do you all have any children?" I told him yes and he said he would have to contact Child Protective Services to do a house call as a standard procedure. It was crazy seeing them cuff her and put her in the back of the police car, but I was too out of it to really give a shit to be honest. Seeing her in the police car at that moment made me realize something - that her and I would never have a physical altercation ever again and so far I'm right. As a matter of fact, I don't even have a fear of her coming at me in that way like I used to in the past. I'll admit that I've had a few sleepless nights not knowing if she was going to attack me or go the fuck off or whatever, but after that day, those fears slowly faded away. From that day forward she knew that I would never respond to her threats or acts of violence and that if something popped off, I was calling 911 and probably moving out of the relationship shortly thereafter.

So, I'm home and Kenya is gone for the night. Edrea is home and my children will be home in a few hours. I needed to lay down and go to sleep. I had to wash my mouth out because it was full of blood. The paramedics asked me if I wanted to go to the hospital, but I said no because that's what I always say when it comes to doctors and the hospital. At that time, my attitude was just let me die in the streets rather than have me laying up in a hospital bed with wires and tubes sticking out of me getting pumped full of meds. No thanks.

I needed Edrea to do two things for me: (1) take care of the kids and the house as if nothing had happened and (2) take my phone and deal with all of my other partners who wanted to talk or come see me. The kids part was no problem because she had already plugged into the family in that way. She was cooking for the kids and cleaning and talking to them and everything. They loved her and could talk to her about almost everything they had going on. It's the girlfriends thing that was going to be new for her and me. I needed her to tell my girlfriends that I wasn't available and that I would get with them in a week or so. I really didn't want them in me and Kenya's business because I didn't feel they had her best interest at heart. They would be biased towards trying to protect me and they probably wouldn't be able to keep their mouths closed when it came to keeping our business private. So I chose to leave them out of the loop and have Edrea be my spokesperson.

Before I explain how she did, there's something you need to know about Edrea. She lacks cooth and her people skills lack refinement to put it mildly. She's quick to curse a motherfucker out. I can hardly even take her out sometimes because she loves to get in someone's face if she thinks they are disrespecting her or not delivering as they should. It could be a waiter, store clerk, bill collector, police officer, or anyone. No one was safe, except for me. I used to love to watch her rip bill collectors a new asshole on the phone. She'd be asking for the supervisor's supervisor. She'd be like, "Ok, you obviously don't know shit about anything. I need to speak to a supervisor who actually has a brain and the ability to do more than repeat scripted lines at me. I'm not trying to offend you, but you're dumb as fuck, which is why you're only making $9.50 and hour. Now please get your boss's boss on the phone and I'll wait as long as it takes. Thank you." I just remember thinking that I never want to be on her bad side. And she would be into it, pacing back and forth with her arms waving while she smoked a blunt. She was so beautiful doing it too. A thick, red bone sister with silky skin blessed by the sun goddess herself cursing out the entire planet. I loved it and I loved her.

So, getting back to the story, my girlfriends started hitting me up one by one and Edrea was on the job intercepting my messages and answering for me when she could and then answer for me when she had to. I heard some of her conversations. Like when Bella called she was like, "He's not available and he can't talk right now. He said, he'll give you a call back next week." Bella was pissed the fuck off. She was like, "What the fuck are you talking about?! Put Rakhem on the fucking phone!" Edrea would be like, "Nope! By hoe!" Edrea came to me and said, "I talked to Bella, but she was pissed. She said she's stopping by the house even though you didn't want her too." I told Edrea to handle it any way she saw fit, but don't let her in the house and I don't want to see her. I mean, my face and mouth was swollen and I had dried blood on my lips and I didnt' want to have to explain anything to her because Bella wasn't a Kenya fan at all. She still blamed her for us not moving in with her years earlier. After about an hour, Bella rolled up to the house and Edrea met her out in the yard. They had a long discussion and eventually Bella drove away. She was pissed though. Man, Edrea was thorough. She really stepped up for me. She handled my other partners as well via text and phone. She talked to Ivory who was also local and wanted to see me without any problem at all.

I could talk to Edrea about all of my other partners. She

would give me advice on how to deal with all of them and let me know what she thought about their intentions. She would tell me if they were running their mouths and who they were talking to. She would tell me who was betraying me and who really loved me and had my back. She was also amazing at defending me online. If she saw someone criticizing me or Kenya online she would go on attack mode and start cursing them the fuck out. I mean, she would go in paragraph after paragraph with the relentless defense of me. She pissed off so many women to where they'll never speak to me again and I was fine with that. If I thought she was out of line, I would tell her to ease up or apologize and she would with no problem. But people learned quickly not to say some sideways shit out their mouth unless they were prepared for a war. Edrea just didn't play that type of shit at all and she was in it to win it.

I could talk to her about her potential lovers. I really wanted her to give another man a chance, but she seemed to think most of them were full of shit or didn't have their shit together. She was just really cautious when it came to other partners.

There was another great quality about Edrea that I liked. Her dedication and loyalty for me included how she interacted with me sexually. There's a reason I mention her with Angelina and Anisah and that's because she took the time to learn what I liked and she gave me that. We literally had sex the exact same way every single night and I loved it. It was some of the best sex I had in my life to that point. It was simple, she would suck my dick perfectly and then ride me until we both orgasmed and then we'd go to sleep. Our sexual connection was so tight that I could even ejaculate during the head she was giving me and she could still get on top of me and come hard as fuck. I loved the way she came too. She would be riding me and she would either fall on top of me or fall off of me. Then we'd cuddle and go to sleep. That was it. No gimmicks. No special positions. No whips, chains, special lube (other than coconut oil), or theatrics. I was in love with her.

But here was the problem - she lived with me and Kenya. That shit just didn't work. I mean, her and Kenya got along great at first because when she moved in, her and I weren't dating. She came into the house as Kenya's personal manager, but of course Kenya knew she liked me and even encouraged us to be together. But still, the shit didn't work after a while because Kenya and I had different philosophies on how open relationships should go. Actually, Kenya was polyamorous and believed in hiearchy and I was open and believed in circular arrangements without any hiearcharchal structures. That was the foundation of the disconnect in the house because Edrea and I had the same philosophy, but it clashed with what Kenya wanted. The long and short of it is those two would end up going at it arguing about who was the queen versus the head queen. Their relationship was rough as fuck and to be honest, I didn't want to deal with two women of different philosophical beliefs trying to coexist in the same house. Plus, I wasn't down with polygyny and this was a perfect example of why. The long and short of it is, I had to make a choice and force a separation of living, which in the end, would end me and Edrea's relationship. I was so sad and hurt by it. It took me years to recover from losing her as a partner. I mean, we would still see each other after she moved out, but it wasn't the same. She shifted her focus on to other things and there really wasn't space for me in her life. I still miss her to this day. I still love her to this day. Our relationship wasn't perfect, but I think we would have had an epic relationship outside of her living with Kenya and I. Like if she had her own place, we would have been great.

This relationship taught me that I couldn't have any partner live with Kenya no matter what anyone said or thought. No matter what Kenya said or thought, I just would never do it ever again. Kenya could have her partner move in, which she did and I was fine with that, but I wouldn't subject any of my partners to being influenced by her or any other of my girlfriends ever again. But I guess I had to go through this experience to know what I wanted, but it's unfortunate that I lost one of my greatest loves to find out.

# The Craziest Bitch on Earth

I wasn't going to write this chapter, but fuck it. Part of my open relating journey was dealing with crazy ass women. I mean, crazy as fuck. I know, I know, they're all reflecting me and my choices, which was especially true in this case. I was an enabler like a motherfucker. I tell this story not to harp on how I was the victim to some crazy bitch who was in love with the "dictacious" but to explain how I learned that persevering through a journey can lead to something mutually beneficial to all parties involved. Kind of like a lessons-learned story for those willing to do the work.

So, the tough thing about dating Southern Bella was that other women saw that relationship and considered it a benchmark of what they could have with Rakhem. They didn't understand that there were special circumstances that allowed for that relationship to flourish and be what it was. It would require that their pussy be as tight and that their voice be as high and penetrating as Bella's. They would need to be as feisty as Bella was, always picking these small fights with me over some philosophical bullshit that didn't matter in the end. It also meant that they had to have an ass as tight as Bella's ass was. If you want your relationship with me to be like mine was with Bella, then you need to have an ass, legs, and thighs that captivated me when you were walking away from me. You have to be able to call my name and have it penetrate my heart for no apparent reason whatsoever. I'm not sure what to tell all these women, but I can't just make myself like or love you the way I love someone else. It doesn't work that way for me. I mean, every time you came during sex, you would have to feed my ego in the same way Bella did. You would have to orgasm every time we had sex, just like Bella did. Your pussy would have to grab my dick and literally hold it hostage for the entire love-making experience just like Bella's did.

There's one problem with convincing some women that everything with them can't be the same as with the other woman - they don't believe it. They refuse to believe it. Some women just want the fantasy, period, point-blank. What's a brother to do? I have women to this day who still use Bella as the benchmark for what we might have one day, and I don't know what to tell them other than it will never be that. Not only because they aren't her, but because I don't want that kind of relationship again. No thanks. Not only that, even though they thought it was all good, the truth is it wasn't. That's just the truth.

So, I had a relationship with a woman who's self-esteem was in the fucking basement. I didn't get into a relationship with her right away because I had zero desire to. My first judgment was that she was batshit crazy, and that assessment would turn out to be correct. Well, kinda. First of all, I wasn't physically attracted to her at all. She wasn't visually appealing in the least to me at that time. I didn't see any sex appeal. Her skin wasn't smooth. Her hands and fingers weren't feminine. She had natural hair, but it was mostly unkempt. A petite body, but just ok. When we finally did have sex, the pussy was just ok. Plus, she wasn't very smart, which is a pet peeve of mine because it makes the relationship more difficult when you have to explain shit over and over again. Her intelligence was kind of weird because, in some areas, she seemed really bright, but when it came to common sense things, she was remedial - like learning disabled. Generally, it was frustrating talking to her, but some conversations would be interesting, especially when she told stories about her past relationships or her time as a sex worker. Good shit.

She persisted, and I eventually obliged, partly because I do believe in the concept of feminine choice. I think that when a woman chooses you, there is something highly beneficial in it for the man being chosen. That turned out to be right, but it was so hard to get there because I lacked attraction to her in all areas.

How was she crazy? She trashed me online, created fake profiles with my name, and contacted all of my friends and associates with my number. She talked shit about me to everyone, especially to other men who were trying to fuck her and hated me because they thought I was fucking half of the Internet. Pretty much every woman who knew me hated her fucking guts. They would be like, "What the fuck is this bitch's problem, Rakhem? Is she that addicted to the dick? What the fuck did you do to her? She's completely gone. A total nutcase." I also lost a lot of pussy because I dated her. I had some really beautiful women tell me they couldn't get with me because they couldn't be associated with someone so unattractive. Like, they couldn't be a part of that kind of harem so-to-speak. It's like it would bring their personal brand down to be grouped in with her as a part of Rakhem's harem. I didn't have a harem, but I totally understood these women's concerns; I wouldn't even bother to try to convince them otherwise. I've felt the same way about women who dated men that I felt were unattractive. I'd be like, I can't really fuck with you because you're out here dating swamp monsters and shit, and I don't want to be associated with that team. She also lacked discipline. Her personal life was in shambles. She had problems handling a lot of life's basics, like taking care of her children or holding a job or keeping a car or paying rent on time. Shit like that. She just wanted to be with me at any cost, She tied her self-worth to the state of our relationship and to how much I liked her. If I was in love with her, it meant she was a worthy human being, but if I didn't, she felt worthless. That was basically it. She wanted what Bella and I had, and she wasn't going to get that shit, which meant she was going to make my life, or at least some part of it, a living hell in the meantime.

I don't want to paint her as being all bad or anything because that wasn't the case. She was just really insecure about her worth as a woman and never had any real success in relationships. She also had a fairly traumatic childhood with one of those overbearing Caribbean mothers who firmly believed in physically and psychologically abusing their children. Plus, her "biological" dad wasn't in the picture at all. Just messy shit that killed her self esteem and self-worth.

It became a project for me to be honest because it tested my masculinity and dominance. I had to be reassuring with her, and I had to find the parts of her to appreciate and find beautiful. I firmly believe all women are beautiful even when they may not strike me as such when I first meet them. It's simply a matter of them finding their beauty. I also think that men can support women in finding their beauty. Once a woman finds her beauty, she starts to glow from the inside out, which in turn affects her physical beauty positively. That is what happened here. Over time, I found myself more and more physically attracted to her.

I found myself very much into her petite frame. She had a nice, tight ass, soft lips, and a beautiful smile. The sex got to be really good too. I liked being on top of that small frame and deep in that pussy. I liked her feminine reactions when I was fucking her well.

But the best lesson I learned was that her insecurity and acting out actually was based on her deep desire for my guidance and leadership as a man. The result was her being super submissive to me. She was literally the most submissive woman whom I've ever dated. A lot of women talk about being submissive, but I've found that it was a rare thing that a woman would actually be in that place consistently and authentically. She would literally do everything for me - cook, massage me, suck me softly and gently for hours. She'd say, "Rakhem, it's time for you to get some head. Would you like your ass licked too." When I was with her, it was literally minimum drama. Actually, it was no drama whatsoever. The only drama that existed was when I wasn't with her. I could stay with her for a week straight and come and go when I wanted without any worries or headaches. She would just text me to see if I wanted breakfast or lunch and then hit me up when it was done. "Dinner is on the table, Rakhem." It was one of my better relationship experiences, to be honest. Being with her was like being on vacation. It was also super easy being with her sexually. She would orgasm just from giving me head. She would orgasm almost immediately after I stuck my hard dick inside of her and then orgasm repeatedly for as long as we fucked. It was effortless. With other women, I would have to work so much harder and fuck them for so long to please them. I'd be like, "Got damn. I'm ready to do something else." I've always appreciated being with women who I naturally and organically aligned with sexually like that. Seamless and effortless.

Being with her was my first experience with being an

acknowledged dominant in a relationship, and it was amazing. She was the kind of woman you can see yourself living with because of how she treated her dominant.

I'm just glad I got to the other side of what I was interpreting as her craziness and acting out. That's all it really was. It was her acting out and pitching a fit to get what she wanted, but she definitely matured over time. I developed in my manhood and masculinity as well. I also really learned to step into the role of a dominant man in relationships, thanks to my relationship with her. She helped me to stop judging women who would act out and look a little deeper to see what was really going on. I'm still not condoning crazy behavior, and it still gets on my fucking nerves. At least now I can empathize and understand there's something deeper happening beneath the surface.

## Isis' Love Spell

I had a woman put a love spell on me. Yes, I believe in those, and yes, they can work if they're done properly. I'm still infatuated by her to this day. I'm still involved with her to this day. No, I'm not mad about the fact she put the love spell on me because love spells feel amazing. It's like being on a narcotic or something, and you're just having euphoric feelings about a woman to the point you'll do anything for her. You'll do anything to be with her. You'll risk it all.

One day this young sister hit me up on messenger, saying that she liked me and wanted to get to know me. She said she'd been following me for years and really liked that I was so open and honest about my lifestyle. I told her thanks, looked at her pictures, and decided that I was attracted to her. From what I could tell, she had a cute little body, with a fat ass, perky breasts, smooth and juicy lips, and a super cute face. Her pictures weren't that prevalent, but she seemed pretty dope from what I could tell. Plus, from talking with her, she was really sexually open. She wanted to suck and fuck me badly and claimed I was the only man that made her feel that way, which was interesting because she was married.

So, we continued to talk on text, and it felt really good. She seemed like a perfect match for me to be honest. She really understood me and wanted to be with me. She said that we were aligned in a lot of ways and that she would take care of me. I liked how that sounded. I still do to this day and am still open to it.

The best way to describe how I felt about her was that I was in love with her. It was different from my other "in love" experiences because the other one's developed slowly over time, but with her, it was instant. The only other time I've experienced falling so deeply and so quickly in love with someone was when I fell in love with Ama while I was living in New York City. I talked about Ama in my book, *Finding Male Sexuality: My Personal Journey in Awakening the Masculine Sexual Self*, so I won't go into it here. The long and short of it was, I fell in love with Ama hard and was ready to divorce Kenya and break up with all my other girlfriends immediately. All it took was one night with her, and I was gone. Well, a similar thing happened with Isis, but it wasn't as intense.

I was in love with her, but I wasn't going to leave my other relationships for her. That said, I was considering moving her in with me even though I didn't want any more women living in the same house as Kenya. I also considered getting her a place really close to me and just tucking her away in my own little world and taking care of her. Still might. Either way, it really caught me off guard when I experienced these feelings for her. I liked her voice too. It was sensual but had a roughness to it as well. It reflected the many challenges she had faced as a young adult, including a high amount of sexual abuse, sexual trafficking, and slavery. It's weird. We hear so much about sex trafficking, but before I met Isis, I had never met anyone who had actually been sex trafficked. I thought her story was incredible because you wonder what actually happens behind the scenes with these people. Like, how do you keep women locked up in a neighborhood without anyone finding out or without them escaping? But hearing her story helped me understand better. It also helped me understand the kind of fucked up abusive shit these women had to go through. I'm sure men were sex trafficked as well, but her story illuminated hers and other women's struggles. Really bad stuff.

So, yeah, her voice and whole demeanor reflected her history. She was sexy but tough at the same time. Really raw around the edges and in a perpetual state of battling those demons from her past.

That whole sex trafficking experience really made it hard for her to love and respect men. As a result, she mostly dated women. I mean, she was married to a man, but she wasn't into him like that. Their marriage was an example of the timing being right for her to get the support she needed to move to the next stage of her life. It's not that she didn't love and appreciate her husband because she did, but he wasn't really able to touch her deeply and connect with her soul. She said he was attempting to be something he wasn't, and it kind of turned her off. Not only that, but he also disrespected her and cheated on her with another woman. That further turned her off from him.

I usually don't fuck with women who are rebounding from a cheating situation with their husband because those situations aren't really about me. They're about revenge and shit like that.

But it was different here because they moved into a polyamorous agreement, so they were both able to date other people. They moved into polyamory because of the cheating, but whatever. Not only do I dislike being with a woman fresh off of her husband cheating on her, but I also don't want to be a married woman's first polyamorous experience either. The existing jealousy from the husband and their overall inexperience is just annoying as fuck. Plus, I have a reputation for fucking a lot of women, which makes it even worse for these husbands. I'd rather just not go there. Go get a few years of dating experience first and then come and hit me up. But I didn't care when it came to her. I was going to get in that pussy if it was the last thing I did. Love spell.

So one day Isis and I are talking, and she says, how about you come to see me this weekend? She lived four hours away from me, which, for me, is a long way. I have other girlfriends in her city, and I wouldn't just drive down to see them because, well, why? I've got options at home, and I'm not big into travel even though I end up doing it a lot. She said she would get a hotel room and everything. All I had to do was come down. I appreciated her offering to get the room, but she didn't have to do that. I would have gotten the room, but she insisted.

As the week moved on, we weren't sure if we were going to be able to see each other. Things were a bit hectic at her home, plus her husband was a nutcase. She told him she was going to fuck me, and he flipped the fuck out. Crying like a bitch online and calling me out like I was violating their marriage or something. It didn't matter because I was going to go up in her. Y'all are officially open, and that's that. Love spell.

So we get to Saturday, and she says, "Come on down, Rakhem. I'll get a room. I'll send you the address to the hotel." I didn't think it was going to happen, and I think I even had other plans, but when she told me to come down, I jumped in the car and rolled. No extra clothes. Kenya was like, "Where are you going?" I'm like, "I'm out and not sure when I'll be back." It was a great drive down to see her. I think it was a new moon or something. I felt really powerful with my spontaneous decision to go see her without a plan.

I get to the hotel, and she's late, of course. So I just sit in the hotel lobby for a while. About forty-five minutes later, she shows up. It was good seeing her again. Yeah, I forgot to mention that I saw her when I was in the city a few months earlier. We had a chance to meet in person. I picked her up from her school, and we hung out and grabbed some coffee or something. She told me she'll do anything for me. I really felt that. So, I got some head in a parking garage. It felt great but left me wanting more, which brings us back to the hotel. So, she starts the check-in process but is having some issues. I send her some cash, and she's able to eventually get checked in. We get to the room, and it's cool. She asks me to excuse her for a second so she can take a phone call. She stepped out into the hallway and I just chilled on the bed. I put both my phones on the nightstand and my laptop bag in the corner and just chilled. She came back into the room and asked if I could go downstairs for a moment because she had to take care of something. She said she'd come downstairs in a second and get me. I'm thinking that's a weird request but obliged nonetheless. The request was so weird that I didn't really think through my next move. I got up and walked out of the room without my phones and laptop bag. I guess I thought I would just be gone for a second or something.

So I step out into the hallway where she was, and she's on a video call with someone. She's holding the phone up, saying, "See! I told you I'm here by myself. Look! No one is here. Now, how do you sound?" I was like, Oh fuck. She must be on the phone with her husband. After seeing that, I walk down the hallway, thinking she needs some time to handle him. Got to the elevator, went downstairs, and decided to go to my car to get some fresh air. So, I'm walking to my car and, all of a sudden, a white car pulls up next to me in the parking lot, and this hip hop dude from the 1980s hops out and yells at me, "I knew it. Who are you here to see? You hear to see my wife?" He's got shades, chains, and a baseball cap on with these perfectly pressed clothes. He was looking like Run DMC for real, though. Or maybe LL Cool J without the muscles. Either way, he was looking kinda clownish. He seemed offended that I didn't know who he was as if I was supposed to remember his profile picture from the bitch post he made a few weeks back. "You here to fuck my wife?" We exchanged a few words, and he marched into the hotel to confront Isis.

Meanwhile, I'm stuck in the parking lot without my phones or computer. I guess I'll just hang out here for a few. While he was gone, I made sure to draw some configurations in the dirt for the deities to come and get some just in case some shit broke out, if you know what I mean. Eventually, they would both come down out of the hotel together, and the three of us would talk. It was beautiful listening to how she was handling her husband, even though she wasn't really getting through to him. "I told you I was going to fuck Rakhem. It's gonna happen. We're fucking, and there's nothing you can do to stop it." I was thinking, "Shit, that was bold." That's some boss chick type of shit right there. He just looked at me like, "Don't fuck my wife, man. There are forces at play that you're not aware of, and if you two hook up, it's going to doom Isis in a way that I can't even explain. You're going to have to trust me on this." In my mind, all I could think about was the fact that we would be fucking, mostly likely before the sun goes down, but I tried to be open-minded. The three of us would eventually go to a food spot and talk things out. The end result was me leaving the city later that afternoon without fucking Isis. I was disappointed but still felt great about her and me. I didn't really care about what he was talking about because they were open. She was honest with him, and he was being kind of an asshole. I mean, tracking her down using her phone GPS to find her at the hotel was kind of a bitch move in my book. Yelling at your wife for her choice in who she wants to fuck while you're out there fucking anyone you want is also a bitch move in my book. I get that polyamory can be difficult, but I don't have much sympathy for guys who act like that. Guys who have a one-sided view on dating where they feel entitled to do whatever they want while simultaneously holding their wife back. Nah, I wasn't feeling it. Plus, I was under Isis' spell anyway. She had me. She could have called me to come back down the next day, and I would have. That's how I was feeling.

We would talk later about everything, and she apologized for her husband's intrusion. I told her I was just fine and we continued to communicate. We would set up another rendezvous a few months later. Same deal except this time I got the hotel in her city and she came through. I got there early and was able to take a nap, which was cool. She came later that evening looking like a cutie. I didn't give her my room number. I just went downstairs and got her when she got to the hotel. That was my precaution in case she and her husband were working together on some weird cat and mouse fetish thing. I mean, it wasn't outside of my mind that they were working together to maybe get me caught up in some bullshit. Yeah, I had been talking to Isis, but in truth, I did't know her that well. So I go and get her and bring her to the room.

She gets comfortable, does some bathroom stuff that women do, and then we get into the sack.

The bottom line is we sucked and fucked, and the pussy was primo. She had this thick ass body that felt amazing to be on top of, underneath, and behind. The head was tight too. I really enjoyed looking down at her breasts, which were perky and just right. Pretty face. It was epic. I eventually came during round two when she was riding me in reverse cowgirl. I think it was just watching her ass go up and down that did it for me. After we were done, she just laughed and said, "You know what you're doing, Rakhem. That dick is good. You're getting these women caught up with that dick, aren't you?" I was just like, I don't know what you're talking about. She was funny that way though. She was always accusing me of knowing the kind of effect I had on women. "How many women have you got caught up, Rakhem? I know it's a lot, right? They don't even know what hit them, right?" I think she was partly just gassing my head up, but she wasn't really a jokester like that, so I'm sure she was at least semi-serious.

We laid around and talked for a bit, and then I suggested we get food. She was down with it and got dressed. We get down to the lobby and walk out into the parking lot. As we turn the corner to head to my car, I see someone standing next to it. As I walk closer, I notice my door is actually open, and someone is going through my car. I see him reach across the driver's side seat, open the glove compartment, pull out some papers, and read through them. Then he starts to look in the back seat. This is all happening as I'm nearing the ninja. When I get closer, I notice it's LL Cool J again. I'm like, "This moutherfucker just doesn't quit. He's full time crazy as a fuck." When I get around to the driver's side of the car, he's standing there with the door open, but he doesn't see me. So I walk up on him.

In my head, I want to punch him in the back of the head and then slam his face into the roof of the car, but then I started calculating repercussions and shit and instead just walked up on him. I said, "What the fuck are you doing in my car, motherfucker?!" He just stood there in shock, looking at me with a crazy-ass, 1980's Run DMC, hip hop deer in the headlights face. I guess he thought I was going to slide him in his face, but it was probably just the shock of getting caught red-handed. He eventually started to mumble some gibberish and move out of the corner I had him in. I literally had him trapped between the open car door and the car. His wife was behind me looking at his dumb ass too. Then he started calling her a cheater and blah, blah, blah. I'm like here we go again with this ninja's shenanigans. Can I just get some quality time alone with his wife or what? Like, can I please bang your wife in peace, bro? Damn!

Actually, I can't say it was like the last time because I made sure to get up in Isis' yoni first before exposing my specific position. I guess he was outside in the parking lot looking for my car and looking through my things while his wife was riding my johnson. I don't know, but I took a picture of his license plate and called the cops anyway because I didn't feel like talking it out this time. He got in his car and took off. I filed a police report. They contacted him, but nothing came of it. I didn't really care. I just wanted to ensure I had some private time with Isis. I just needed him on record as being a creepy, sleazy moutherfucker just in case some real shit broke out later.

Apart from that, Isis and I had a great time for the rest of the night. We got breakfast the next morning and talked things through. I dropped her off at the house, and our relationship was consummated. I'm sure LL Cool J gave her a hard time, but she assured me that she knew how to handle him. I was like, cool. So everything was good until she started getting vague about birth control, ovulation, and shit like that. That's one thing I will admit is that I never got a clear response from her on what she did for birth control. I thought she said something about her not being able to get pregnant, but I really don't know what the fuck she said. I think that's how the love spell works - it makes everything vague as a motherfucker. So I'm talking to her one day, and we're talking about the sex, and she says, "Well, no one is going to tell me whether to have a baby or not." I was like, what did she just say? Like, where did that come from? Here we go on some crazy shit. You talk about sweating bullets. I was stressed like a motherfucker when she started talking about pregnancy and shit. I was in love with her and under a spell, but I wasn't in a coma. How the fuck would that work - her having a baby and being married to a crazy, bitchmade motherfucker like her husband. Jesus take the wheel in this motherfucker. It took me about two months to calm down after that, but all I could do was my own personal work and talk to my sperm and tell them to stand the fuck down. Please and thank you. That is all. She turned out not to be pregnant, but that kind of snapped me out of the love spell. I was like, "What are you doing with your life Rakhem?!"

I would eventually talk with the husband on the phone, and we got to a decent place. Not a good place, but cordial. I'd say we were at about a five out of ten on the scale of cool. It was during this conversation that he told me Isis put a love spell on me. That's how I found out. He said, "You know she put a love spell on you, right?" That's when all my behavior started to make sense. I was still into her though. Isis and I would have our ups and downs after that, but we've been able to stay connected. She's super dedicated to me, and I love that about her. I love her consistency.

Later he would turn into one of those men who would "follow me," meaning he would begin to contact the women I was dating and attempt to talk to them. Some dudes have a fetish like that where they're attracted to the women of a man they "despise" (i.e., love), and they try to have sex with her. My first experience like that was in college when this dude tried to fuck my college sweetheart. He was kind of upset at me because he didn't get into my fraternity. I guess he held me partly responsible for that, so he wanted to fuck my girl to get me back. My girl told me all about it and said he was obsessed or something. She didn't give him any pussy once she saw where he was coming from. Anyway, there will be more chapters to this story, but we'll have to wait and see.

But here's the kicker. While this was going on, one of my other girlfriends, The Craziest Bitch in the World, somehow found out about my obsession with Isis. She somehow started talking to Isis' husband because he was, of course, "interested" (i.e., following me) in her. The Craziest Bitch starts coming at me crazy as fuck saying I'm going to run away with Isis and stop seeing all of my other girlfriends. She's freaking out about us not being able to see each other anymore because I'm going to be with Isis. She's all in my inbox, crying and texting me pages and paragraphs of messages. I'm like, "Ain't this a bitch for real?!" Of all the motherfuckers I wouldn't want to get wind of what I got going on with Isis, Crazy Hoe had to find out and start tripping all over the fucking Internet. Just being messy as fuck. It was a total embarrassment. I was ashamed that I was actually dating her. I felt like a fucking fool for going through some crazy ass shit with her before and still being willing to date her. And so here I was again, having to deal with a total nut job. I basically had to cut her off and not talk to her for a month until she could read a book and get some sense or something. She eventually calmed down and I could move into a new, tamer chapter with Isis going forward. We're still connected, but we'll have to see what happens.

## The Trouble with Erin

It appears that I can't add "specialness" or other monogamous principles to my open relating life. There's just no room for it. The way I open relate calls for a series of organically generated relationships without any one of them taking precedence over the other. There will always be favorites, but they are all equal in terms of their impact on my life. This seems to be my charge and lifestyle based on who I actually am and what I desire to experience out of life. I'm a firm believer in people relating in a way that aligns with their soul level. That is why I prefer an open relationship over polyamory or other structures. Who I am can't really be put into a box; there has to be room for change and adjustment throughout the rest of my life. There has to be room for trial and error, mistakes, failures, and total resets without me having to feel I've violated a tenet of my stated relationship preference. Open relating for me means organically relating with others while having complete, unapologetic acceptance of myself in the process. It is loving myself and others unconditionally and without judgment to the absolute best of my ability. That's the only thing that works for me in the long run. Unattached love. Non-possessive love. Non-ownership-based love. Complete acceptance of the individual without mandatorily forced rules or protocols that, in the end, are only designed to protect the ego part of ourselves. Another way to say it is, "You do you, and I'll do me." I'll love you fiercely, completely, and vulnerably without owning or restricting you while demanding you do the same for me. It's doing what feels absolutely amazing for me and supporting you in doing the exact same for yourself, even if that means you do it without me. Yes, it's love, but it's the warmongering part of love that takes no prisoners. It doesn't allow itself to be used as a tool of manipulation or coercion to rob other people's freedom or manipulate them into codependency. It's the warlike love that doesn't allow the ego to get too high on itself at the expense of honoring the entire self - mind, body, and spirit. I don't buy into the concept of love only being gentle and kind and subject to being walked all over by the bullies of the world - hate, jealousy, envy, insecurity, greed, possessiveness, duplicity, self-denial, or unworthiness. No, love fights back and kicks ass until she wins the day handily. No prisoners. No quitting. No compromising. No excuses. Yeah, that's my love, and she's sexy as a motherfucker, and she's a rider until the day I leave the planet and take a new form of my choosing the next go around.

But why am I writing now after being in an open marriage for well over a decade? And furthermore, how am I arriving at this conclusion that my love expression must be rooted in the purest form of love for me to stay sane inside of my relationship experiences?

## The Dream

This morning around 2:20 am, I awoke from a dream. The dream was about my partner and her partner and the fact that they just met up in a city nearby to see each other. When I texted her, she told me she had gone out of town, but she didn't say she was meeting anyone. That was fine because it's none of my business. However, because I am pursuing a deeper relationship with her, one which could potentially diminish my other relationships, I am hyper-sensitive about what she does, who she dates, etc. As I said in the prologue, "specialness" and monogamous principles will put a person in that state of mind whether they want to or not. The dream shed light on the fact that she went to see a partner she dated before me and is still dating to this day, although with somewhat less intensity. Let's go back in time a bit.

She made the first contact, expressing an interest in dating me. Shortly after that, she suddenly disappeared for no apparent reason. I began investigating why. It wasn't anything super serious, but it was definitely something I was interested in understanding. I thought her disappearance had to do with me venting about another partner of mine. It was an intense and crushing commentary about The Craziest Bitch on Earth. My ego went in very hard on her and it affected the way other women started to view me. They saw another side of me that they didn't know had previously existed. But that wasn't the reason she disappeared. My research indicated that she was dating someone else who is a popular, high profile personality in our community. The look of their relationship seemed very intense and very connected. She had told me in another conversation that they would talk for hours every day. I found that they had done many live videos together over a series of months. I concluded there wasn't the time or serious interest for me to be in her life based on the intensity and seriousness of this other relationship.

Was that an issue? No, it was not. At least not in a vacuum, but it would be significant later. Their relationship appeared to last for about a year in a semi-exclusive and intense state. They continued to see each other after that, but it seemed the intensity died down. How did I reach that conclusion? The fact that she reached back out to me after all of these months. Hmm...it appears that she has an interest in me, but is that all that it is. Perhaps it's that her previous relationship didn't work out the way she wanted it to, which was to see more time, growth, and increased bonding. This is a common occurrence in relationships. If one partner is looking for things to grow into something more committed, intense, and serious, but it doesn't happen, they often bail on the relationship. I recently had a partner break up with me for the same exact reason, so I get it.

So, what do we have here? A potential rebound scenario? A possible situation where if you can't have what you really want, then settle for the next best thing? I can't be exactly sure, but it does beg the question. Plus, when I look at the other evidence, the case seems to be even stronger. As she and I have bonded since dating each other, she has been liberal in sharing her relationship history - the good, the bad, and the miscellaneous. She shared a story about a guy she liked, and that she wanted to have a serious, committed relationship with him. She indicated their time together was amazing, connected, and intense, but he didn't want a serious relationship, either with her or probably anyone at that time. Apparently, this is still his stance, but her interest in him remains. The point is, I see a pattern developing - her liking a guy, wanting a serious committed relationship with him, the guy not giving it to her, and her moving on to the next guy. In theory, that pattern isn't a red flag. It's what most people end up doing until they find someone who will commit with them. However, on another level, it might just be a red flag if one of the previous partners was and is her true love. Meaning, if one of her previous partners is the man she really, really wanted to be with then, that's exactly where her heart is going to be. It will be with him and not with her current boyfriend, which right now would be me.

I asked her about her relationship with her previous guy (the one she ghosted me for) and why things had changed. She said it was because he was on his "guru" thing, and she didn't want to be a part of that reality. What exactly does that mean? It didn't sound accurate to me in terms of explaining why they wouldn't be together anymore. In another conversation, she told me that they naturally and organically stopped talking as much and things just naturally faded away between them. In other words, he stopped showing the same level of interest and backed out of the relationship slowly. She must have understood what was going on and allowed it to happen so as to not make a fool of herself by trying to keep him in her life when he obviously had a change of heart. That seemed more likely to me - he stepped away from her. If so, is her heart still with him? Because if it is, he could step back into the situation at any time. I'm not saying it would be a seamless reintroduction back into her life as a fully committed and intense partner like they used to be. That would depend on putting in the time to match the desire.

So, back to the actual dream. I dreamed about her going to see him. There was a narrator who commented on her dating scenario. He was saying how she was amazed at how her three partners had big, girthy penises, and that she couldn't get enough of them. She was excited at the prospect of having these three partners in her life and appeared to be really in love with her previous partner. The identity of the third partner wasn't clear in the dream.

The shock of that dream and realization that she went to see him, woke me up, and I wasn't able to get back to sleep. It started me on a thinking spree, trying to make sense of everything. I felt like a "red pill" guy who was trying not to be played. It was like all the progressive and open mindset went out the window, and I was caught up in recounting the rules of the game. It was a tough place to be.

From one standpoint, I was thinking that I would merely ignore all of these thoughts and information and just focus on our relationship. I mean, I'm dating a ton of women and just met some new ones that I'd like to follow up with. It shouldn't really matter what she does or who she loves, but it did. Why? Because of "specialness." If I simply stay in the mental, emotional, and relationship zone that I've been in for the past five years, then I wouldn't have anything to worry about. I would do me, she would do her, and we would come together when we came together. No discussions on living together. No extra considerations of time and deeper connection. Instead, just allowing things to flow without trying to make plans or declare specialness in the relationship. But I didn't stay in that place when it came to her. I allowed myself to go deeper with her and cultivate a level of specialness that caused me to be in my head all the time when it came to our relationship. It's not where I wanted to be, but too late. I was already there.

Oh yeah. So, how did I verify that she went out of town to see him? Simple. I verified his travel schedule. Low and behold, he was in the same city she was traveling to. Dream substantiated. I guess sometimes dreams are pinpoint accurate. The scary part about the accuracy was that I had to consider the other aspects of the dream as well, where she declared her intense love for him. The kind of love that seemed to trump what she felt for me. The kind of love that made it seem as though we were only together because it was the next best option. The kind of love that she didn't want to end, and if it were up to her, they would still be together in an intense relationship just like before. Except that she would also be away from her baby's father, who is the common denominator in these scenarios.

You see, when she was with her previous two partners, she was also with her baby's father. But that relationship wasn't fulfilling for her. According to her, it also was kind of abusive, mentally and emotionally. She would manipulate him and he would cave to all of her demands eventually. She confirmed this with me during our many talks about him and her past relationships, but it was also kind of obvious to see from the outside looking in. She was living with her baby's daddy, and I'm sure that added to the monotony of the relationship, which is why she introduced open relating to their relationship - against his wishes, I might add. He wasn't down for it and actually confronted her previous partner before backing down and accepting it.

The mental and emotional abuse (manipulation) is a red flag, but it's hard to take it seriously because she made me feel like I was an exception to that kind of behavior. Maybe I am. And I'm not saying I've experienced that myself, but the real question is - would I clearly see it if it was happening to me? It's hard to say. My ego would obviously like to believe so, but I can't be too sure. Maybe she is currently manipulating me as indicated by the fact that I'm willing to go further into a committed partnership with her than her previous two partners were. What did they see that I'm not seeing? Is her previous partner coming back into the picture simply because I'm dating and getting closer to her now? Is that what is making him think he might have made a mistake in letting her go? Maybe me being with her is causing him to question his judgment so now he must go back and reassess the situation. I kind of saw this happen actually. She posted a picture online and she was looking super hot. He commented and clearly displayed a desire to get reacquainted with her. But at that time,

I really didn't know the depth of their relationship. I mean, I knew they dated, but I didn't realize how serious it was until I did the research.

I would say, technically, she's still in a relationship with her baby daddy even though she lives alone now. That means I can't really say I'm in a different position than her two previous partners. It's like she's keeping him around as a backup plan until she finds and secures something better. I'm not saying this is the actual plan, but it just seems like it. Again, he'll do whatever she tells him to do eventually. He's not even mad at me anymore for dating her, which I never really understood in the first place, but whatever. It's like, dude, she's been dating guys and trying to get away from you way before I came in the picture. Maybe he just sees Kenya and me as the authors of open relating and responsible for her dating other men in general. Perhaps it's because he had a coaching session with me about his relationship with her, and he thought that meant I would never date her. I can see that, I guess. But as I said earlier, I don't do preemptive "bro code" strikes.

The other part that disturbed me about her visiting him was a series of assumptions that I made about that trip - the biggest one being that she paid for it. Again, I'm not saying that's the case, but I am saying that's the assumption. It's hard to see it any other way, but I'm sure there are other options like him sending her the money to rent the car. But, the fact that she rented a car with her money and drove down there and back irks me because everything that she and I do is on my dime. It makes me feel like more of a sucker. It makes me feel like I'm being played. I don't know, it just hurts.

But this entire insight, the scenario and feelings I'm describing, doesn't make any sense unless I acknowledge the thorn in my mind underlying my relationship with her and the mental challenges that I'm having with her. What is that? Well, a number of months ago, I had one of my partners in town for a weekend visit. She's one of my friendly girlfriends who likes to meet people, and she wanted to meet Erin. So, I invited Erin to the house to meet her and everything went great. They seemed to get along well and ended up developing a friendship. I must say that I don't know if that was a good move on my part. It violated one of my relationship tenets - always keep partners separate from one another unless they initiate contact with each other and develop their own bond. I firmly believe in that. Fast forward to later that night, Erin and her partner at the time come back to the house to hang out with Kenya and her partner. My partner and I didn't hang with them because she had to catch an early flight the next morning, so we were in bed by 9pm. Long story short, Kenya, her partner, Erin, and her partner end up having a foursome in Kenya's room, and they were loud as fuck. So, I'm basically listening to Erin, the girlfriend I'm toying with being in love with, fucking Kenya's partner. That felt like shit and has ended up haunting me ever since. As a matter of fact, it severely delayed my desire to get closer to her because I didn't want to be with someone who would fuck a dude right across the hall from me. Trust me, I get that a lot of people are into that kind of lifestyle where fucking whoever, wherever, whenever, even when your other partners are around, is the norm. I'm just not a part of that culture. I would never fuck her roommate in the next room in front of her like that and on top of that be loud as fuck. It's just not my principle. That was and continues to be hurtful, and as I'm writing this, it reminds me of why I most likely can't be closer to her than where we are now. I just can't go all-in when someone has that set of values. And I'm not saying she did anything malicious, although I'm not discounting it. I'm just saying, I'm not down with it.

How could it have been malicious, and why? Maybe she was bothered by me introducing her to my other partner. Perhaps she thought I was rubbing her face in it. Maybe she was jealous and fucked my wife's partner in the next room super loud as a way to get back at me. It's certainly not that far fetched, especially considering how loud she was and for how long she was loud. I mean, Kenya said later that she was mad at her partner because he came so quick when he was inside of Erin so where exactly was all the noise coming from? Was it her partner that was fucking her that good that long? Because if it was, she needs to stay with his ass because he was putting it down. Why be with me because I'm not fucking you all night like that. And maybe it was the combination of both of those brothers, and that's why it was so long. I don't know if I believe that either because Kenya was in the room too, and I know she wasn't just sitting there watching Erin get all the dick all night. But hey, anything is possible right? So, yeah. I'm still salty about that episode, and to me, it shows a quality of character that I shouldn't ignore.

What's interesting is that my partner Monie Love told me not to date Erin. I thought it was because Erin was talking about our relationship business to another member of a mutual women's group and that her baby daddy hated me. Erin was communicating all of that to this other sister and the other sister told my partner Monie Love everything. But I need to circle back to Monie Love and ask her if there is a specific reason she thinks I shouldn't date Erin. Is there a quality of character issue? Because Monie's strength is looking at people's character as indicated by their behavior. She's got a low tolerance for people who act shady or who can't be trusted. This might be something she saw in Erin.

I mean, that was definitely a part of it because she didn't like how Erin was telling all of our relationship business, but there may be more there.

But there's also a chance that Monie Love was overblowing things to keep me away from Erin. Why? Well, Erin has an incredible body, and I think she knows it; whereas, Monie Love doesn't necessarily have the same level of confidence about her body. She might also have felt that I was more into Erin because I hadn't been spending as much time with her after Erin moved locally. Erin might have been viewed as a threat to us building anything deeper. As a matter of fact, it was probably safe to assume that she felt I was more into Erin than I was her. These are the types of things I've had to deal with when it comes to having multiple partners - competition and insecurity. How do you manage all of these personalities, needs, desires, and insecurities with their place in my life? It's not easy, and I've gotten my fair share of bumps and bruises over the years in trying to manage multiple relationships. The first thing I decided was that I needed to keep all my partners separate. I wasn't going to bring partners together to meet or for friendship unless they initiated with one another first. I can't say that I've been successful with this one, but I'm above ninety-five percent for sure. You have to understand, for me, it's about managing an overactive mind with a predisposition for finding the worst possible scenario or a justification for our negative feelings about ourselves. I should know because I suffer from the same thing myself. My mind can run wild if it's not properly checked. I'll come up with all kinds of scenarios for what a partner is or isn't doing or what they meant on a social media post or whatever. Yes, this is based on my insecurity, but it's also a part of the human condition, particularly for those raised in a western culture founded in resource scarcity. That's a long, drawn-out way of saying that it's not just a symptom of a woman's mind, but of the human mind, especially when it comes to relationships where our personal value is often derived from how someone else treats us.

I'm not a believer in the common polyamorous philosophy of all parties and partners being friends and forming a happy community of support for one another. I mean, I know it's possible, and I've heard of those types of relationships existing, but they're not appealing to me. Many of them are overly laden with rules and protocols to protect people's feelings and egos. They also lack passion, and what's the point of relating with someone if the passion isn't there? I mean, the exception is, of course, when you're living with someone for the long term as it's expected that the monotony of life and upholding the foundation of a living space will zap people of energy and passion. Outside of domestication, I'm not down for drudgery, chore, and obligatory relating. I would have just stayed in monogamy if I wanted that. So let's keep everyone in their own little corners of the world. Let me focus on each individual relationship as its own complete experience without the need to validate it with the approval of other partners or by the upholding of a utopian version of open relating. Not only that, but when partners come together in shared environments, it's expected that certain personalities will tend to dominate and have an influence over others. There's also a chance that some partners may become obsessed with comparisons and start to feel insecure about their position relative to other partners. I mean, that's human nature, right? To look at other people and compare how they're being treated or the quality of their connection to others. This can be disastrous because each connection I have with the women in my life is different, which again is the point of having multiple partners -

so I can have multiple, varying experiences that are fulfilling and unique. The last thing I want is one of my girlfriends trying to make our relationship look like someone else's. If that's the case, then why be with you, right? I'll just be with her.

So that was the dream. That was the realization that helped me get my mind right and keep me on a path of being open, free, general, and away from monogamous relationship principles. It doesn't change how I feel about Erin. I still love her deeply and will continue to spend a lot of quality time with her, just like I'm doing now. But I won't be making future plans. I won't be thinking about exclusivity on any level (not that that was ever expected of me, but that's how I was beginning to think). Stay open and free.

So I had to ask myself, how much of this is simply jealousy versus a true concern about Erin's character and values matching up with mine. Or is this "concern" really my fear she might be playing me or might be settling for me because she is truly in love with another man (or men) who won't settle down with her? It's hard to say. I must assume there is some jealousy playing out in my mind and heart, which is why I'm feeling the way I'm feeling and why I'm doing the investigation I've been doing. When you look at my behavior, it's just too typical of jealousy and insecurity to not say those elements don't exist. That said, I don't think it's all about jealousy. As a matter of fact, I don't think it's mostly about jealousy either. I think I do have legitimate concerns as I move into the next phase of my life where I seek to build a solid bond with a woman who understands me and will nurture, take care of, and protect me going forward. I felt I had this bond with Edrea, but haven't had it with anyone since her. She was a true ride or die partner who would be mindful of protecting my feelings whenever she could. She had sense like that, and now I realize that's a rare quality to find in people.

I guess I should take the time to qualify something because my description may sound as if I'm seeking shallow connections with women, and that's not the case. Yes, indeed, I'm saying that deep connections bring out feelings of jealousy and insecurity, and thus I want to avoid them. That doesn't mean I don't have deep connections because I do. I love all of my partners very deeply. I enjoy our sex life, our time talking and spending time together, and everything we do and build together like projects, business stuff, and ways to make money. To me, this is depth, but without ownership and possessiveness. It allows a sense of freedom and autonomy while also knowing you have a strong support network in the form of a community of people who love you. That's what I have, and I love that. The deep love I was referring to is possessive love. It's a love that says you're mine and simply sets us up for failure.

As I mentioned before, I'm wishing to avoid "specialness." Meaning, where I believe there is something about me in her heart that transcends all other men on the planet right now and in perpetuity. First of all, there's no way that could be true, and second of all, there's no way that could be true. Why set myself up for a letdown by believing in a false narrative about myself as seen through another person. In my mind, the proper perspective is to house that specialness inside of my own heart and mind, so that way, I'm not burdening her or anyone else to have to maintain that narrative. It's too much pressure to ask her to avoid meeting anyone else for the rest of her life who is also just as special as me or even more so. I don't have to be more special than all her exes or future lovers or whatever. So, that's the difference. I'm not saying others shouldn't engage in special love, but it's just not the path for me at this stage in my life. Maybe I'll revisit my stance at a later time just like I did in this relationship and decide to pursue the specialness path. Who knows?

But there's more to the story that could help me unpack whether I'm a jealous mess or really analyzing if a situation is best for me at this time. The sex was amazing. She basically mastered me and my penis and even told me about myself. "Yeah, Rakhem. When you get hard, your penis turns red here and here. Also, the vein on the top of your penis expands. I can even feel your pulse through that vein when it's in my mouth, and it's not a weak pulse. It's super strong." I asked the obvious question, "Can you feel my pulse when it's in your vagina?" She gave me the answer I wanted to hear, "Yes. Yes, I can." In my opinion, sex doesn't complicate relationships, but mind-blowing sex definitely does. Any time there's an intense pleasure factor involved in a situation, it will be more difficult to rationalize things. It'll be more difficult to think clearly. Not only that, but I believe amazing, mind-blowing sex rewires your mind and makes the source of that sex, Erin, in this case, a focus of what you create in your life. It's hard to forget extreme pleasure. Not only that, but Erin has an amazing body. Fat ass, perky titties, thick legs, thick lips, brown skin, soft feet, and great style. She's easy on the eyes, to say the least, and mesmerizing to say the most. I love watching her ass when she walks away from the bed or down the hallway. But yeah, the sex is exceptional for me. Great match. She knows how to get me excited and aroused. She's willing to give in the form of massages, lingam massages, head, dick riding, and nipple stimulation. That's all my shit right there, and she knows it. Sigh. You want to communicate with your partners so they know what to do to please you during sex. When they become a little to proficient at it, you sometimes find yourself digging an emotional hole. Now they're doing the puppet string thing and dangling pleasure in front of you even if only subconsciously.

So, I consider myself to be a bit of a lazy lover. Don't get me wrong, I'm willing to put in work, but I really like to lay back and receive. I'll lay back, and she'll give me a lingam massage and head for about forty-five minutes, then get on top of me and ride me for another forty-five minutes or whenever I ejaculate. I like that, but it can get a little too intense sometimes because she rides and stimulates me at the same time so I can feel my brain starting to check out or at least get rewired. It feels amazing, but it is also a form of pain just because of the intensity. And I'm talking real shit here. Like she's driving me crazy while she's riding my dick. I'm squirming and moaning like I'm getting appendix surgery without anesthesia. If I didn't have a dope sexual experience with Edrea, where I learned to be vulnerable and loud, it might even be a traumatic experience for me. When Edrea used to give me head, I felt like I was about to lose my fucking mind. She was similar to Erin in that she studied my body and really learned what I liked, needed, and wanted. She was the only woman I was with where I could come in her mouth, then she could get on top of me, and my dick stayed hard until she nutted. It was like the way her pussy fit around my dick made it stay hard enough to have a full sexual experience after I came. I was always amazed by that. So here I go manifesting a similar situation with Erin. Both Edrea and Erin are submissive, adaptable, creative, and super smart. They can literally figure out a way out of no way, and that skill comes in real handy during sex. Getting back to Erin, it's funny because she told me about some of her past sexual experiences, and some were physically violent in nature. She used to choke ninjas and shit, which is amazing considering she's so fucking small, but small girls usually are the first to fight, so I guess it's no surprise.

Her riding me caused me to come hard every time, but me being on top of her had the same effect. I always came hard on top of her in a missionary position, but it was better because she could come in that position too. Sometimes it was hard figuring out when she was coming unless she told me. Part of the reason is that she was usually loud and screaming throughout most of our intercourse experience anyway. Not only that but when I eat her pussy out, she ends up coming super hard, leaving no fucking doubt whatsoever. Then her clitoris gets super sensitive, and I just put my mouth over it without touching it. I might gently blow on it for a while before I start to lick it gently. Like, really, really gently to slowly bring feeling and pleasure back into her clit again. What's great is I can do the slow and gentle touch with her clit and vulva for about thirty minutes and then get back to eating her pussy again, and she'll come again super hard. I love that. I tend to eat pussy only one way, and that's using a gentle finesse. I really dislike having to suck a clit really aggressively for it to feel something. I guess that comes from everyone's unique biology and maybe over aggressive masturbation, but whatever the reason, I'm not trying to eat those pussies. Get a Scorpio or Cancer man to do that. I'm a Gemini, and eating pussy is a gentle art for me. So it's big for me to find a partner who responds well to the way I eat pussy and the way I make love. I mean, I consider myself to be gentle, but Erin is consistently telling me to slow down and be gentle. My partner Anisah used to tell me the same thing. She'd be like, "Rakhem, I like that slow glide of your dick going in and out of my pussy." Kenya may have even told me that back in the day. Kenya used to tell everyone that I was a thrasher in the bedroom. I couldn't believe it when I first heard her say it. I was like, "WTF?!" I always saw myself as gentle and smooth with my stroke, but maybe it wasn't even about my thrusting speed, but the fact my dick is so girthy. Because of the extra girth, I probably need to go more slowly than if my penis were a bit thinner. And my dick is fat according to the women I've dated. I've had over twenty women tell me my dick is the thickest dick they've ever seen, so I guess there's some truth to it. Whatever. Anisah also told me my dick was super smooth, and that allowed for easy entry into her pussy. She was like, "Rakhem, you have the smoothest penis I've ever seen. It slides right in my pussy." It's confusing. The bottom line is I need to make sure I'm going slowly with Erin and Anisah even though partners like Anita love when I aggressively thrust in and out of that pussy. But she's a Cancer so I can see her loving it aggressively. Cancer and Scorpio women love to go hard sexually. They're not really into the finesse sex like Geminis, Pisces, and some Aquarius women.

But I digress. The bottom line is the sex between Erin and me was top-notch. I'm sure that contributes to my confusing feelings about her. Jealousy and insecurity is a hell of a drug.

## My Work

There are two sides to every coin, right? The other side that makes "the dream" scary is that I have my own patterns. I have a history of being with women who want more from me only for me not to deliver and for that relationship to end in a breakup. As I mentioned earlier, I just went through a breakup where that happened to me. My ex-partner was expecting that we spend about two days a week together, and I couldn't meet that expectation with her. Actually, I never thought I made that commitment, but I believe she had that belief. The fact that I can't say for sure what she was expecting is a red flag for any woman looking for long term commitment from me. It's just not a priority for me or even something I desire, except, maybe secretly, I do a little. I do desire that ride or die partner, where we have an amazing connection just like Edrea, but circumstances, along with an inability to find that person, have prevented me from duplicating what I once had. There's always something that doesn't seem to be aligned. For example, with Erin, the character and values difference is at the core of the mismatch. Usually, I would say it was her children, but she's established a scenario where her children aren't living with her. That has nothing to do with me, but more about the freedom she desires for herself. The point is that I'm at the stage in my life where certain circumstances aren't going to be workable.

You see, when I was with Edrea, all of the circumstances seemed to be aligned. She was childless, we had similar viewpoints, and we were super sexually aligned where all we did was suck and ride. She believed in my work and my talents and was willing to work and contribute money. Although she was jealous, she managed to keep it in check and channel it into making our relationship stronger. Those are just a few. She was also the first woman in my lifetime that I can remember consistently offering me head during the daytime. "Do you want some head, Rakhem?" It would hurt me to refuse it, but I only refused because of our living circumstances. We were living in a communal setting with my wife and children and didn't have enough privacy to really make things work. That brings me to another point - romance without finance is a nuisance in the words of Big Daddy Kane, but we'll come back to that later.

My partner Cidney called it the SHAMS. She said, "Rakhem, my sister told me to avoid the SHAMS at all costs, and I think you should do the same." I said, "What are the SHAMS?" She said, "That's short for SHAMBLES. When someone's life is in shambles, you'll have to avoid getting involved in that situation. You'll have to let them be and figure it out for themselves so that you don't get dragged down in the muck and mire of it all." I ended up taking on that philosophy and avoiding situations that didn't align with freedom and my desired lifestyle. One SHAM was children. It's not that I don't love children in general, but I'm not trying to be around them. I have three of my own; one is a sophomore in high school while the other two are out of the house trying to figure life out. I just don't want to go down that path again. Children kill your happiness unless you've adopted a passion for parenting. It has to be your life, in my opinion; otherwise, you're resentful and continually looking for escape mechanisms to find time for yourself.

I've always said that I believe children are the number one cause of divorce in America. It's not that having children is inherently wrong. It's that the demands of raising them in a nuclear family environment, day in and day out for twenty plus years, can be too much for a couple. The pressure and stress can lead to divorce. Of course, that's just my opinion. I know most people don't agree with me because it's sacrilegious to speak "negatively" about children in any way or claim they are a source of stress in an adult relationship. But that's what I believe. The most stated reasons for divorce are finances and a lack of communication. To me, both are greatly affected by the presence of children in the house. They cost two-hundred and fifty thousand dollars each to raise. They dominate the narrative in the house; that is, most of the communication is around them and what to do with them. It's just a thought.

The SHAMS is not just about children, but any situation where people's shit isn't together in such a way that it would take me away from my joy and goals in life. For example, one of my partners is Isis. Great pussy, beautiful sister, loves me to death, and wants to be with me. But has a jealous husband who's the definition of a cockblocker. I talked about her earlier. I still want to be with her, but I don't have time to be with a woman who doesn't have her man in check. I don't have time to deal with jealous ninjas who are pussy whipped and insecure about their ability to be a real man out here in these dating streets. She's got the SHAMS because of her husband. She's also got the SHAMS because she doesn't have a place for us to be when I come down to visit her. It's like, what's up with these women without a place to fuck?

That's like my girl, Elysia, on the west coast. Every time I go to see her, I'm spending two grand on food and lodging, so I just can't be with her like that anymore. I mean, a ticket across the country, hotel or Airbnb, Uber X, and food adds up. I might as well have just gone to the islands and got some real smog-free sun and a beach without freezing cold Pacific water that I have to wear a wetsuit for. That's the SHAMS. I can't do anything with that based on where I'm trying to go and what I'm trying to do. It's nothing personal against her. If she had her own place, I would probably be with her, as in living with her, and might even consider being exclusive with her. Who knows, but the point is these are examples of the SHAMS. I've got my own SHAMS to deal with (just like all of us), I can't be taking on other people's SHAMS too. I know some women look at me in the same way like, "Um, no. Rakhem has a whole wife and thirty plus girlfriends. I don't want to deal with all of that." I totally get it and no offense taken at all because I'm the same exact way.

The great thing about Erin is she has her own place and no

children living with her. She's got her baby daddy in check. She's got no roommates. She makes her own money and needs very little help from me even though I'm sure she's hitting up other ninjas, but that ain't my business either just like who she's fucking ain't my business either.

But I digress. What am I going to do about my patterns? When I combine my failed specialness and exclusive commitments with Erin's past of not getting what she wants from men, it doesn't take a genius to see the train wreck coming. Epic failure with a whole lotta pain is a very likely scenario. So the question became whether to work to resolve my own personal patterns or to continue to live my life as I had been. As stated before, I've chosen the latter. There's no need to resolve that pattern per se because I currently exist in a twenty-four-year marriage with my wife, Kenya. Yes, that marriage has changed over time, and we aren't having sex for going on three years now, but none of those things are negatives in my book. We're better friends than ever and getting along really well. In addition to that, we've been really productive with our business and maintaining the household. No arguments (well, very few and very, very low intensity when it does happen) and no physical fights. I'll take that any day considering our history.

But what are my other patterns? I know in the introduction of this manuscript I described the kind of love that I needed to be my best self and to maintain a level of sanity in my relationships, But like I said, "Love is war." I need to fight against my inner need to feel special inside of relationships. I need to fight against my deep desire for my partners to be "in love" with me as a way for me to boost my ego. The ego is tricky, and it manipulates situations to gain what it wants. Or another way to say it is - I manipulate situations in order to get what my ego wants. Yep, let's call Rakhem out so we can get firmly out of victim and blame mode for a second.

I know the dick is good, and I use that to gain favor with women, but I have another quality that's even more sinister. I'm a chameleon of sorts. I can be what any woman needs me to be to facilitate her falling in love with me. It's not a skill unique to me. Actually, all VISIONARY minded people have this skill, including Erin. That is why I find my mind all fucked up over her. She molded herself into exactly what I wanted and needed, and that caused me to covet her and be possessive and crazy over her. What's good for the goose is good for the gander, right? I guess you can say we fucked each other into vulnerable and needy states of "special" love for one another. I know Erin is in love with me, but for me, that's par for the course. I totally expect women to be in love with me because of how I show up in their lives. It's just a part of my personality, and I do it wherever I go including in work environments. I just make the adjustment. I become the team player or the ultimate follower or the ultimate leader, depending on what the situation demands. Again, it's a VISIONARY characteristic to be able to change with the times and the environments we find ourselves in.

But there's a problem with me functioning this way. That behavior usually can't be sustained over the long term because I end up denying myself what I want when I'm in a constant state of adjusting. It just doesn't work because her love is now based on the adjustment I made to accommodate her and make her feel good, and it was never meant to be that way. The accommodation is simply a way to allow us to break the ice and connect without our guards being up. Well, that's how it's supposed to work, but yes, I enjoy the fact that it draws a woman's love towards me. It feels good, but it's all my ego, and it's my responsibility to manage it correctly. Because what happens when a woman falls in love with me is she starts thinking of ways to get me to fall in love with her. I have a partner who's been obsessively stuck in that pattern for years. She wants me to be deeply in love with her because she's in love with me. In other words, she's attempting to feed her ego in the same exact way I fed mine, and it becomes toxic for the relationship. It turns into an exercise in relationship survival for her. The only way she can win (be happy in the relationship) is if she secures the ultimate prize of having me, Rakhem Seku, deeply in love with her. That is, when I prioritize her, in terms of time, energy, money, and public declaration, over every other woman in my life. That's the opposite of non-possessive love and love that is unconditional.

It's so hard to have the ability to be everything to a woman and have her either fall in love with you or even simply love you deeply and not do that. I battle with it every day. I hold back my tantric powers so that the energy of simply being around me isn't too intoxicating. I encourage my partners to find other partners to spend time with and be in a primary relationship with. But when my ego wins, it's hard for me to pull back. I pull them in and establish a deep love connection.

The funny thing is Erin told me this was her superpower. She told me she knows how to be what a man needs, and based on how her ex-partners were acting, I believe her. These dudes are crazy as a motherfucker. Stalkers, willing to do whatever, and open to being manipulated. It's a sad sight to behold. What's even worse is watching myself become one of those motherfuckers. Jesus take the wheel here and save me before I'm out here in the streets losing alpha male points. The last thing I want to do is to be analyzing text messages, social media statuses, and trying to put two and two together to add up to five. I don't want to be a researcher or investigator. I don't want to be up all night in my head or in the case with Erin waking up out of my sleep to a dream giving me insights on her whereabouts the previous weekend. It sucks, and the only way out of it is to stop doing the same shit myself and get back to the kind of love that keeps me balanced.

But what I'm essentially saying is that dating Erin is like dating myself and guess what? I don't think I would date Rakhem Seku. This motherfucker is a handful. What I'm experiencing with her is what many of the women who've dated me are experiencing. How so? Well, I've fucked partners in front of each other before. Yeah, the circumstances may have been slightly different, but let's admit it - it's the same thing. I'm sure the partners who were within earshot were like, "I would like to kill this motherfucker right now." I've incited jealousy in my partners. I've displayed and demonstrated questionable values. That was one of Bella's big complaints about me. She would say, "What do you actually stand for Rakhem? Is no one in your life special and worth protecting?" Bella was my first girlfriend to make me see that I wasn't protecting my partner's feelings and emotions, and that included Kenya. When I look back at my behavior inside of open relating, it was clear that many of my choices and actions were very hurtful to Kenya. Things done in poor taste and things that appeared to lack integrity. And I'm not just talking about things behind the scenes, but public events and social media postings. So, I get it. No one is doing anything to me. I'm simply dating myself as I date Erin. I'll probably be able to resolve my feelings and issues with her once I learn to love and accept myself. Or maybe I need to heal the traumas that cause me to not consider others more carefully and deliberately. I can't say for sure, but I know I have work to do. I also know that Erin is a sweetie and is simply showing me who I am.

Can I get an Amen? How about an Ase'. And so it is.

## The Queen Anita

Anita was the most beautiful woman I've ever dated. Beautiful brown skin and a killer body. Locs. Gorgeous smile and a total sweetie. Every time we went out, I would look at her and say, "That's what God looks like when she manifests in the flesh here upon the planet Earth." The sex was amazing too. She was so accommodating to me and my needs that it made each and every experience with her so pleasant, free, and easy. But more on that later.

I'd rather talk about my insecurities when it came to Anita because that's what's most relevant in these open relating scenarios. Sure, we all know about the good times when things are new and easy, but what makes open relating difficult are the challenges that trigger our fears and insecurities. Anita had a husband and a boyfriend. You would think the husband was the main issue, but no, it was actually the boyfriend. She and the boyfriend had been together for over a decade and had a well-established relationship. He wanted to be with her exclusively as in marriage once her children were grown and out of the house. Did I mention that she wasn't in an open marriage with her husband? No? OK, well, she wasn't when I came into the picture. She was officially monogamous with her husband, and her boyfriend was on the side, so to speak. I guess they had a master plan of being together, and he was way more possessive than the husband could ever be. That said, she and her husband were also well-established with a great family. You could actually see them staying together and her continuing to date on the side. It's hard to say, but it's certainly a possibility. In summary, that makes me the third wheel for real. For real. I'm like the side piece to the side piece, which wouldn't matter so much if I didn't care for her so much. I'm not sure why I was so shocked by how much I was into her. Maybe it was her beauty. Actually, I couldn't believe she didn't have more men in her life who were complete paid out baller types. She's that thorough, in my opinion. Maybe it's because she's kind of nerdy and just coming into her own as a beautiful, sexual, independent woman who no longer needed to play mother. She's a professional and connects with a lot of high powered executives. I don't know. It's just interesting that she was available in the way she was.

So what's the dilemma? Is it an ego thing that I'm her number three or maybe even lower? Nope. It's that I really love her and had thoughts of being with her. How does that work when you're number three on the totem pole behind two men who collectively have almost forty years of time and history with her? Well, usually it doesn't work for the third man. Usually, it is a two-man battle between the husband and the number one boyfriend.

I was also insecure about my financial situation. You see, Kenya's and my finances are tied together in our business. For me to be with Anita, even on a semi-permanent basis, I would need a new source of income completely separate from my business with Kenya. But wouldn't that be an issue with anyone else I may choose to be with in a domestic living situation, even if it was only part-time? The answer is yes for many, but not all of my partners. I date a lot of women. Many of them would be perfectly fine supporting me while I got on my feet without any problem whatsoever. Food, shelter, and amenities would be all covered.

Car access, you name it. And to a degree, I would expect that because of the work I've put in on myself over the years. I would hope they would hold me in high regard and see my energy and presence as enough of a contribution. I mean, women find themselves in that situation all the time. I'm all about leveling the playing field when it comes to what we can expect for ourselves as human beings, so why not? Not only that, but I'm already domesticated to handle chores and responsibilities. There's no way I would actually be in a domestic living situation without pulling my weight. It's just great to know that I have partners who are willing to support me in that way. It feels incredible, actually.

But back to Anita. She's a bit more high class and corporate-oriented than a lot of my other partners. I'm sure she would an expect equal monetary contribution, at least. Especially because I hear her complaining all the time about how she has to carry an extra financial burden in her marriage. It's something that she's attracted into her life - men not pulling their weight. It wouldn't sit right for me to approach her in that way if I wasn't ready to contribute out the gate even though I'm sure she would do it just so we could be together. Sometimes it's hard to admit that my finances aren't where I'd like them to be, but in terms of supporting an additional household, it's true in my case. I'd have to get to work. I guess this is what they mean when they say women force you to bring out your best self when you're in a relationship with them because she definitely has me wanting to be better.

As a side note, at any given time, I might be dating thirty-plus women at a time. I didn't even realize how many women I was dating until I started getting asked that question by interviewers on television shows and radio outlets. This lady on the Dr. Phil Show™ was pressing me. The number was so high and sporadic that I couldn't even calculate it the moment she asked the question. I had to redefine in my head what a girlfriend (or partner) even was. I settled on the number five after telling her repeatedly I had zero idea. But dating women is an expensive endeavor. Travel. Dates. Help with bills. Coffee. Gas. Hotels. I mean, you name it. Even for someone like me, who insists that women bring some kind of financial substance to the table, it can still add up. Dating multiple women consistently is not a poor man's game, that's for sure. The good thing about it is it helps you stay on top of your money game. But there's another benefit to having to pay money to date multiples. It helps you focus on the women who really like and love you because they are willing to do what's required to make the relationship work. That's big, especially when you look at the other reality, which is some women expect to be treated because they feel entitled. I just can't rock with women like that because I know my value as a man, healer, and solid brother all the way around. I'm not out to prove anything to someone who's feeling entitled. I paid for almost everything when it came to dating Anita, and I was happy to do it because she was incredible in all ways. I mean, I would have done it anyway in most other scenarios, but she was a dime. True goddess type ish.

Here's the thing - I was kind of surprised that our interaction was so seamless. I almost didn't trust it, to be honest, because sometimes women try very hard, in the beginning, to have that perfect face on so that you'll like them. I guess those thoughts were in the back of my mind, but not in a heavy way. I was really just more appreciative of how we could interact together without forcing anything and without any drama. That was partly because she had been married for over two decades and was my age. There was a level of experience and maturity with her that I usually didn't experience with women because my partners were usually ten years or so younger than me. Yeah, I guess the word I would use is maturity on her part. It's like she just got it when it came to the basics. She understood that life is too short for bullshit. If you like and love someone, it's best to just focus on that and leave the insignificant crap for the youngsters to tussle over.

There was something much deeper at play that I found to be totally profound, deep, and beautiful at the same time. She had the same Bagua Character Map (a type of astrological chart) as my mother. The Bagua Character Map is broken down into three parts: MIND (how you think), SPIRIT (your emotional state), and BODY (how you feel physically). That was a big deal for me because I did a lot of work to heal my relationship with my mother and release any resentments I had towards her. Things like her and my biological father getting a divorce when I was seven years old. Just whatever because I'm a part of the generation that blames their parents and others for their lives. When we became adults, we assumed that our failures in life, whether in relationships or in finances, had something to do with what our parents didn't do for us. That was very real for me because when I decided that I wanted to get married, I made a conscious declaration that I didn't want a woman like my mother. Part of it was that I felt my mother was a nag and over bossy when it came to my life. Later I found out that it was simply a trait of Cancer women to want to run other people's lives and have their input be heard for their own sanity. It wasn't anything personal coming from my mom because, of course, she just wanted the best for me. Still, as a child, it was annoying as fuck and overbearing at times. All I could think about was not wanting a woman who would be like that to me in marriage.

I wanted someone more pleasant and amenable. Unfortunately, I didn't know shit about astrology until I was about fifteen years into my marriage with Kenya, who is also a Cancer woman. Low and behold - I married my mother anyway. There's a saying about that, right? You can't run away from yourself. Or everywhere you go, there you are. Anyway, I had to learn to deal with that Cancer energy through my wife. Did I master it? No, but I made significant progress. Well, I continued to do the work, including some with my mother, and that really helped. We became good friends, and I'm happy with our relationship to this day.

Well, my wife, Kenya, only shared one trait with my mother. That was the Cancer Sun sign, or in the Bagua Character Map, it was that she had a SOLDIER body. Anita's three traits were all the same as my mother's, and guess what? We got along great, which for me, was a sign that I truly did have total acceptance and appreciation for my mother and that the healing work was successful. I mean, I really wanted to be with Anita. I could see myself living with her and everything, which is big for me because I'm not easy to live with. I want what I want and need alone time, even when you're in the house with me. I want sex my way. I expect financial contribution and some meals cooked. Plus, I'll be dating a lot of women and still probably be in my feelings when you date other men just like I was with Erin. Crazy, isn't it? So, yeah, I'm not the easiest person to live with. Typical Gemini type stuff, but that said, I'm a really sweet and thoughtful guy with common sense and excellent domestic training. Great sense of humor. You'll never have to take out the trash, etc.

I can't tell you how happy I was to hear that Anita had my mother's same astrological chart. I mean, I learned about this after we had been spending time together, talking, and supporting one another. I have to admit that I had reservations about Anita when I found out early on that she was a Cancer, but things worked out nicely. Actually, the fact that things worked out so nicely and the fact that she had my mother's same chart made me feel more confident in being with her than any other partner I was dating. Part of it is my astrology nerdiness, I'm sure, but trust me, this was a beautiful revelation.

Anita is not only physically beautiful, but she treats me beautifully. She loves me and takes care of me. She considers me and my happiness. She's careful with me. She fucks me thoroughly and completely and makes sure I'm stimulated and pleased. She makes sure I get the rest I need. She cuddles with me even when it gets hot and sweaty under the sheets. She tells me what she wants - "Rakhem, suck my pussy, and put your fingers in me." She sucks me after I come inside her pussy, which was a first for me. Part of her logic was that my dick fits better in her mouth after it's gone soft a bit. All I know is it's such a nurturing offering from her. It feels special. She sucks me soft with her whole mouth and keeps her mouth open a little so that my dick is caressed in her wetness. She sits on my face and does the riding until she nuts, but she'll also stimulate me at the same time to keep me intense and engaged. Her smile makes me smile. It's so bright like a summer afternoon. Her laugh is infectious to the point where the only time I don't want to see her smiling is when I'm deep inside of her looking down upon her beautiful face as she tries to navigate my girth pushing inside of her and expanding her walls. She holds my hand when we walk even though her husband and boyfriend are roaming the city too. She gifts me her body so that I can worship it and experience the love of the goddess first hand. I love her, and she loves me. She's vulnerable with me and tells me her worries with her husband and her boyfriend when she knows she can't talk to them about how she really feels. I hold a special place in her heart as the only man she can tell absolutely everything to. Every time we make love, she gives it everything she has. She throws the pussy at me regardless of the position. When I'm behind her, she throws her ass at me and pushes off the headboard to maximize her thrusting power. She moans, pushes, and grunts like it's leg day at the gym. The pussy feels like silk. I wondered how a woman over a foot shorter than me can have a pussy that caresses my dick perfectly. We use coconut oil, but we don't need it because her pussy calls for my dick, and my dick longs for her insides. Her appreciation of me is always said in her words and communicated in her facial expressions and voice inflections. I never doubt my place with her, even though my insecurities might try to tell me otherwise. She reassures me that I'm worthy and special and a man she loves for all eternity. I want that. I pray for that. What would it be like to be in a committed relationship with a goddess herself? Is that a life of worship, or is that a life of learning to match her perfection. She teaches me to always be in my joy and to move towards my ecstasy. How can I ever repay her? I can respect her as a woman of class and power. I can please her sexually in all ways that I can. I can stroke her and hold my ejaculation until she is wet and fulfilled. All of this, after I make her come hard through oral and vaginal stimulation. I love her. Isn't it obvious?

I want to be number one in her heart. Her boyfriend is possessive, antiquated, and delusional. He actually thinks he can have her to himself. Ridiculous right? Actually, dumb as fuck. Don't get me wrong; I appreciate him expanding her out of depression and the monotony of her marriage. She wasn't happy. She needed passion, sex, and someone who would love her. I honor that. Thank you. But that doesn't get you exclusive rights to her pussy. All you did was start the process of freeing the powerful feminine energy inside her. Now she's an insatiable goddess who needs to be fed twenty-four hours per day and seven days a week. She truly is insatiable. I would never try to keep her to myself although my ego would love it. My ego would love to claim her as all mine and watch other ninjas look at me as I walk through the city holding her hand. I see them checking out her perfect ass and hips. I see them captivated by her perfect skin tone. I see them intrigued by her wavy hair swaying in the wind. I see them being frozen in their shoes when they look into her eyes. She's like a Kemetic goddess of power and love. Actually, she's like a combination of Oya and Oshun. She enjoys the time we spend together at the restaurant and at the mall and in the car. But in the back of her eyes is the constant question that she sends, penetrating my soul, "When are you going to suck and fuck me into oblivion Rakhem? I want to feel you inside of me. Can you take me to bed now? Right now?! Don't worry. I'm patient, and I will wait, but I want you to know that I don't want to wait."

Anita exudes sexual energy, but she did an amazing job of hiding it from the masses of people. How did she do it? Through smiles and giggles and an engaging friendliness that can easily lead to stimulating conversations. I don't think it can actually be hidden, though. All the men can see it. They all want her, but few dare to approach her because her energy is so strong that it's intimidating. Her coworkers know that she is married, but they don't know that she's necessarily open to new connections. It is what it is. When we went to dinner at a nice restaurant, she was late getting there because of traffic. I was anticipating her arrival, but it wasn't a date per se, just us meeting up. She wanted to talk about some relationship things with me and perhaps get some coaching from me. She had come to my event a few days before and was engaged. It felt good having her there.

When she did arrive, she looked perfect. I was basically in love with her immediately, even though I didn't even know her or her situation. She wore a green, loose-fitting dress that stopped well above the knees. It was tightened snugly to her waist by a belt and delicately cradled her breasts, giving them plenty of room to breathe and flow. Her hair was perfect. I could tell she was a little anxious about being late to our dinner date. I didn't care because I was so excited about seeing her. I wanted to hold her hand once she got out of the car, but I refrained because I felt she needed to settle down a bit and gather herself. We went into the restaurant. It was packed, but there was still available seating. We sat at a booth. I sat across from her. This was my first time at the restaurant, but she had been there plenty of times. We talked about her children and her job. She was wondering if it might be good for her children to get some coaching as they got ready to transition to the next phase of their adult lives. Before she could go further, I reached for her hand and held it from across the table. She looked at me and smiled. She was obviously surprised, but pleasantly so. I wanted to make sure she knew I was interested in her and had a desire to be close to her. From that point on, the conversation shifted to us, and that was the beginning of our relationship. It was such a blessing.

## Ivory's Pussy

Ivory broke up with me, which really isn't anything new. She's done that before because I didn't make myself available to her enough. I didn't come through enough. I wasn't consistent enough. I wasn't communicative enough and so on and so forth. That's the story of my life - women wanting more of my time and energy and me being oblivious to those needs and desires. What can I say? It's basically who I am. When I was dating Southern

Bella, it was different. She was a Libra, and into the fantasy of relationships from all the romance novels she read as a youth. She locked into me with an amazing voice, petite frame, and the tightest pussy in the south. She battled me every day for consistency and focus. She took that responsibility on herself, and I came around pretty good. When a woman is willing to put the work in to get me aligned to their relationship fantasy, I can fit in, but if they leave it to me to initiate calls and special moments, then I fail horribly. It is what it is, but the tight pussy helped keep me focused on Bella. The beautiful eyes and energy helped me stay focused on Diamond as she pressed me for consistency.

That said, Ivory didn't like to call me or contact me or initiate much. She was one of my only partners who truly let me do all the initiating in the relationship. If I didn't call her, we just wouldn't be talking. I could go weeks without contacting her, and she wouldn't check on me or text me, "WTF Rakhem?!" She'd just let it ride out until I got my shit together. This came in handy in certain respects, like when I was traveling or with other partners. I never had to worry about checking on her or having to send that obligatory text message or whatever, which was good for me because I hate obligation, and I hate having to focus on a partner when I'm already with one. I mean, I'll do it, but I don't want to be forced to do it.

So, apparently, we hit that "last straw" point in the relationship, and she cut me loose. It was a sad day, but I totally get where she was coming from and don't judge her decision at all. I really loved her and appreciated how she showed up for me. I loved her children and her story. It was all love. That said, I guess I knew that it couldn't really work because of the logistics of it all. As I mentioned earlier, I'm always open to expanding my relationships with any of my partners. I had gotten to the point where I was considering moving in with another of my partners temporarily. It's hard to say how long I would have lived with her, but I was seriously willing to give it a try because I believed there could be great value in growing closer to partners in certain relationships as a way to (a) facilitate my work and career, (b) to support them in getting on their feet financially, and (c) to become more connected in the relationship. I had a few prerequisites, though. The sexual connection had to be perfect, there couldn't be any SHAMS that were too hard to overcome that would make the arrangement unrealistic, my partners needed to have a place for me as in a house or apartment with enough space for me, and they needed to understand that I need alone time even when I'm in the house for meditating, writing, thinking, and just recalibrating. I wouldn't need a man cave per se, but I would need to be left alone. Edrea did a magnificent job of giving me space when we lived together. We could be in the house together all day and not speak until ten o'clock that night. It was perfect. Well, Ivory only met one of my four prerequisites. Can you guess which one it was? Ding, ding, ding! Correct. It was the perfect sexual connection. Jesus Christ that pussy was good as a motherfucker man. You talk about a perfect fit for my girthy penis. She had it. Plus, she stayed wet like a bucket full of oily silk rags. A-MAY-ZING!! The pussy was so good that I was thinking of how I could get around the other three prerequisites without selling myself out. I was getting ready to raise kids and everything, and that is my fucking nemesis. I have three children, two of whom are out of the house, and I'm not trying to go back there for nothing. But I was thinking about it. Talking myself into it. Talking myself into living somewhere where I was guaranteed to not have any privacy or at least very little. I mean, we're talking about a substantial decrease in my quality of living to make this scenario work, but I was willing to give it a shot.

At that time, I had four women I was willing to consider living with part-time, and Ivory was one of them. In reality, only two of them had adequate living arrangements. And really only one of them would be able to meet all four prerequisites. Anita was one, but she was married and living with her husband. Ivory had a house full of children and no place or space for me. Sierra was working on her living arrangements but was probably going to need help from me to make it work so I could live there, and that wasn't super appealing, to be honest. Now, if she was able to secure her spot, I think we would have been good. We didn't have a lot of sexual experience to that point, but I suspected that it would be fire. She was totally service focused and believed in the sacred suck and ride practice. Her head was amazing too. She did that slow suck and found the sensitive veins and areas on my penis and would focus on that. I was pretty amazed at that, actually. I'd be like, "What the fuck is she doing down there that's making this head feel so amazing? Like, what's her strategy here to stop and keep my penis in her mouth and then work her tongue on the area under the bottom of the head of my penis?" It was amazing shit. Erin was a possibility as well, but at the time, we weren't quite as connected as we are now, where I'm basically pussy whipped or whatever.

The long and short of it was that three of the four partners met either three or all four prerequisites plus no children in the house, but I was still leaning towards Ivory. As a matter of fact, the very last time we had sex, I remember being deep in that pussy, and the only word that I could think of was "Wife." I was about to say to her, "You're my fucking wife! I'm so serious right now." Man, oh, man. That breaks one of my biggest rules ever - never say shit to a woman or make any promises or declarations to her while you're in the pussy or before you've ejaculated. You just don't do it because men aren't all there when we're in the pussy raw. We're just not. I mean, it's one of the most vulnerable places for us to be in. We're literally crazy. That's where all these children are coming from because we're not thinking rationally or logically when we're in the pussy raw. It's not the same when I'm wearing a condom because that latex barrier prevents me from losing my soul to the pussy, but when I'm raw, you can forget it. Mind gone and don't let the pussy be exceptional because then it's a wrap for real. These were the types of thoughts I would have every time I was in Ivory's pussy. Not that I was thinking about her being my wife every time, but I would be in total awe every time and would be thinking about the future.

One of the things that amazed me about my sexual connection with Ivory was that we really didn't have sex that often. I really only saw her like once or twice a month, and to be honest, I never understood that. I have no earthly idea why I wasn't in that pussy every day. It was one of the world's greatest unsolved mysteries. I mean, I'm sure there's a reason, but it never made any sense to me. Maybe it was the fact that the environment didn't really support me being over there and comfortable outside of sex and sleep. Actually, the sleeping scenario wasn't the greatest either because of the neighborhood she lived in. Her room and bed were great, but the people around her were on the loud side, and there was too much lighting outside to block with the shades. Nothing to overshadow the fact the pussy was top shelf, but maybe enough to make it tough to get there regularly.

This goes to the core of where I was at this point in my life. The truth is sexual connection is so very critical for me. A dope sexual connection gives me life like nothing else on the planet can. Raw, ejaculatory sex, where I can keep my penis resting inside the yoni until it naturally falls out, gives me power. It's my youth potion. It keeps me young and my hair black. When I'm done having sex, I'm up and energized. When I used to have sex with condoms, I would be tired as fuck after sex. Drained like a motherfucker, needing time to reset. That's not the case now. Now, I'm up, awake with a clear mind. Yeah, I might take a short rest because of the cardio workout of me pumping and grinding in the pussy and working out my abdominal muscles. Yeah, a cardio workout will make anyone tired, but that's a different tired from being drained from losing semen during sex. I know so many men who are exhausted after sex like I used to be. That's the opposite of what they should be experiencing. Pussy gives you life, man. It's the fountain of youth. Sure, my dick will go soft after I ejaculate, but my mind is clear and crisp and ready to go. She might be asleep, but I'm awake. I'm up thinking, pondering, planning, and loving life. Combine sitting in the pussy after ejaculation with soft kissing and a dimepiece caressing your back, and you experience the true healing powers of the goddess. Shit, it's like being in the womb again. I had plenty of those moments with Ivory.

One of the things I loved about Ivory was that I was naturally aroused by her. It wasn't about physical attraction, but just having a desire to have sex with her. She was one of my few partners who I would get hard for without much stimulation, which is saying a lot considering the number of partners I have had and the fact that I rarely feel like having sex. Horniness is rarely a driver for me wanting to have sex. Generally, my partners bring that out of me and cause me to want to have sex with them. My general disposition in life is to feel satiated when it comes to sex. I guess the best example would be if I eat a nice steak dinner at 5pm, I feel like it's about 7:30 or 8pm. I feel like I could eat, but if I go to bed, I'm still cool. I remember the days when I was starving for sex, and that's some painful stuff. You consider doing a lot of things to get that satiated feeling like masturbating, calling an ex-girlfriend, or making a bad decision leaving the club at four in the morning. Another way to say it is, I would be ready to have sex with Ivory the quickest out of all my partners. Like, I could walk into her bedroom, strip my clothes off, get on top of her, and be inside of her ten seconds later. That's not my usual modus operandi. I usually need some foreplay or something to get me fully aroused.

I probably had the strongest overall attraction to her out of all of my partners. It was just something about who she was as a sexual being and her pretty eyes, lips, and hands. Jesus, I loved her hands and fingernails. That shit turned me on. The same goes for her toes too. I think that a weakness I have for women is hand and feet presentation with the rings, nail paint, ankle bracelets, the shape and softness of their hands and feet, and the list goes on. Putting a woman's legs in the air while I have her in missionary and looking to the side and seeing pretty ass feet just makes my dick harder. Or looking down and seeing her hands on my chest while I'm on top of her and inside of her makes me start to melt away. That's one of the things that got me more into Erin when I noticed her wearing some dark blue toenail polish with the ankle bracelets and then feeling how fucking soft her feet were. But Ivory had my favorite hands and feet out of all my current partners. I would compliment her on them every time I saw her. "I like your nails, Ivory." She would always respond with a high pitched, "Thank you." I would be thinking to myself, "You know exactly what you're doing when you get your nails done like that. You know I like that shit." Not only do I like seeing feet in the air or hands on my chest, but I love to watch soft, pretty fingers wrapped around my penis. I don't even need to be receiving any head. It just looks amazing, like that's where fingers are supposed to be. Right there wrapped around my penis. I think I'll get some professional pictures taken of various women's fingers wrapped around my cock. That would be cool as shit.

But I wouldn't be complete if I didn't say the last thing I loved about Ivory, and that was the way she gently licked my balls. That shit felt so Goddamn good that I can't even explain it. Her mouth was so beautiful and delicate. Her tongue was always gentle in how it engaged me, which was perfect for testicular stimulation because my balls are so sensitive. Like, if woman attempted to suck my balls, I would probably pass the fuck out or writhe in pain. Either one, but Ivory had this super gentle licking motion she would do, and that got my dick hard as fuck.

So let me give out some history here in terms of my discovery into testicular stimulation. I went to get a massage from an Asian massage parlor when I was on a business trip. I really didn't know much about massage parlors to be perfectly honest, but I was stressed the fuck out from traveling and needed to be touched and soothed physically. So, I'm on the table laying down butt naked on my stomach with a towel over me, and the nice lady starts giving me a massage. She starts at the shoulders and moves down the back and arms. Just standard stuff, no biggie, but it was feeling great, and it was just what I needed. Here's where things got interesting. She moved down to my buttocks, and I was surprised that she went a bit far into the crack of my ass. Again, I didn't have any experience at a massage parlor, so I had no idea what to expect. It was cool, though. Next, she worked down from the top of my left leg all the way to my feet then came back to the top of my buttocks for another run down my leg. But this time, she went to my inner thigh and ran her hand down my leg from the inside.

When she started the inner leg part of the massage, she barely swiped my nutsack. It was so slight of a stroke that I swore it was by accident, but it felt so fucking good that it caught me off guard. It was like I felt this tingling sensation that I had never felt before, and then I had a slight urge to pee. From that moment on, I was in my head because that was the best feeling that I had had in years. When she came back up, she did it again; gently swiping my nutsack with her fingertips as she ran her hands down my leg. This made the feeling in my testicles even more intense. The vibration increased, and my feeling of having to urinate all of a sudden became something that had to be addressed. Like I was going to have to get up and use the restroom in the middle of the massage type of urgency. But instead, I just laid on the table and enjoyed the feeling while also being bewildered as fuck about what was going on. It was like I was being gently sexually violated or something without really knowing it. It was my own personal little #metoo moment and was a total mindfuck. Then she went down the other leg - top of the right leg first, then the inner leg next. Same thing, the tip of her fingers gently stroking my nutsack. When she did it another time, I actually ejaculated on the table. I literally shot semen out of my penis onto the towel I was laying on. I was embarrassed as fuck and tried to be as discreet as I could while simultaneously closing my legs so that my penis was out of her view. I literally had to suppress my joy and be quiet and still while semen was shooting out of my penis. I couldn't believe that I came, but I also couldn't believe that my testicles were that sensitive to pleasure where they could be stroked so gently to make me cum like that. Now, maybe I was super backed up from a lack of sex because I had been traveling so much and not really having sex consistently or getting that much touch. Maybe that made me extra sensitive to her touch. I really don't know, but that was an eye-opener. The massage lady moved to my feet, but I told her that I needed to use the restroom. When I was in the bathroom, I looked at my penis in disbelief. I wiped myself off and tried to gather myself as best I could. I urinated, washed my hands, and got back onto the table, but before I did, I looked to see what kind of semen stain I left. It was barely noticeable, but it was there for sure. To this day, I wasn't sure if she knew I came or not, but I would have to believe that she did. I mean, how could you not know, especially, with me getting up to go to the bathroom like that.

Ivory's testicle licking brought me back to that experience, and I almost had a similar reaction. It was nowhere near as strong as what I experienced during the massage, but the gentleness and amazing feeling were definitely comparable. I really enjoyed and appreciated her gentleness with my testicles because my sensitivity makes me very conscious of how women touch me. But here's what was also interesting - she carried her testicle licking technique over to my penis, and it wasn't working at all. My penis needed way more stimulation. I mean, soft head is the shit, but it can't be those gentle licks that she used on my balls. My cock is way more resilient than that and needs way more engagement. It's funny how those things work, but what it told me is the penis and testicles are two totally different animals when it comes to sex for me. Do not, in any circumstance, treat my dick like you do my balls and vice versa.

I've already said that I was sad about the breakup and that I do miss her, but this brings me to an important question. How connected I am to my partners and how much hurt I experience when something like this happens? I wonder if I may be in denial about the level of heartache I feel around Ivory not being in my life anymore. She was essentially my best sex partner when it was all said and done, and we got along really, really well. It's a bad habit for men to sometimes downplay their emotional connection to a woman, especially one as sweet to me as Ivory. So let me take the time to list all the things I miss and appreciate about her and give thanks for having her in my life for a season.

I'm grateful for her beautiful spirit. She was always willing to accommodate me and work with me as best she could. I appreciate the time she took to study my astrological chart and to try to know me on a metaphysical level. I value the interest she showed in my work and metaphysical perspective on life. She would always acknowledge my views and the work I did, and that felt amazing. I appreciate her being in touch with me from a psychic and energetical perspective to the point where she knew what was going on with me even when we weren't physically together. I appreciated her being flexible when it came time to go out to eat. She was so adorable in acting like she didn't have a preference for what she wanted to eat when I knew she really wanted to get pad Thai or hit her favorite vegan restaurant. She was always so accommodating whenever I stayed at her house. She tried to make me comfortable as best she could and would even put off watching her favorite shows to spend time with me. I appreciate her beautiful mouth. It was so pleasant to look at and amazing to kiss. I appreciate her willingness to come to me even when she had other responsibilities. I'm grateful she gave us a try even though it was a long shot because of the distance and the sheer odds of her actually being able to get what she wanted in a relationship with me. I appreciate that she took the time to understand my wife and was respectful of her feelings and needs. That's something that most women really don't understand when it comes to considering the emotions and pressures of a married woman who's sharing her husband with other women. She understood because she had been in that position herself.

I'm grateful that she trusted me to get to know her children. That meant a lot. I appreciate her sharing stories and experiences about her and her ex-husband. I really learned a lot about her and her mindset through that. I valued the fact that she always focused on finding empowerment for herself and women alike. I know a part of that came from the bad experience she had in her marriage with a man who was a part of a heavily patriarchal, religious group, but it was still admirable to see her strive for her personal empowerment. I appreciated her defending me to her mother, who was always skeptical about her life and choices. I'm grateful for her tenderness. I'm grateful for her willingness to make moves to ensure our long-term future together. I admire her resilience. She accomplished so much through her sheer will to succeed, and that's a rare quality for anyone to have, let alone a single woman. I really loved that she was a theater nerd and into movies, acting, and artsy stuff. I appreciate her sexual authenticity and vulnerability. She had a purity about her that made sex with her sacred and enjoyable. I appreciate her willingness to be open to change. It was the only way we were able to last as long as we did.

I'll miss her and always love her.

# Monie's Magnetism

I stated earlier that Monie Love was street smart. She would watch people and identify their character. She always said that loyalty was the most important thing for her. That was her biggest issue with a lot of my partners; she felt they weren't loyal to me. She'd say, "Loyalty is a big deal to me, Rakhem, so when women are talking loosely about you, I take it personally. Why are they putting your business out in the streets to people who don't even care about you? I just feel that certain things should be kept in house." That was her big issue with Erin. She heard that Erin would tell her baby's father negative things about me, which would make him pissed at me and would potentially put me in danger. "I just don't like women like that, Rakhem. I've seen ninjas get killed because women would run their mouth to the wrong person. I'm just scared for you, that's all. I really do love and care for you, Rakhem."

It takes a while to get to know people. For a long time, I didn't really believe Monie Love was being totally authentic when she would tell me stuff like that. I thought she was just trying to increase her position relative to the new girlfriend in my life because she was scared she might be replaced in some kind of way. I've had women do that in the past where they would paint another woman in a negative light to make them look bad in my eyes. I mean, it didn't happen a lot, but it has happened. They would be quick to tell me who else one of my girlfriends is fucking or what my girlfriend said about me behind my back or whatever. The problem with hearing information like this is it's hard to ignore and get out of your head. I can ignore it or put it in context, but you can't unhear it. You can't avoid analyzing that information to see if there is any truth to it. From that standpoint, I kind of resented getting that type of information because it became my burden to carry and deal with. When I'm sitting there with my girlfriend who I just got this information about, I can't be totally free and easy with her because I'm wondering if there's any truth to what I've heard. I want to ask her about it, but then I have to consider if she'll be honest. If she is talking about me, then why would she admit it? Right, a mind fuck. So, I changed my philosophy to not really care what women say or do when they're not around me. They could be trashing me to all their girlfriends, saying, "Rakhem's dick is super duper tiny." I don't really care as long as you're showing up in my life in the right way when I'm with you. As long as I'm not experiencing negative energy from you or experiencing a loss of some kind from being with you, it just doesn't matter to me. Say what you want, do what you want. Just make sure that when we're together, you're on point.

So, I really learned to appreciate her insights and wisdom. I also enjoyed listening to her stories about her past relationships, especially the ones with women. She taught me a lot about lesbian culture since that was most of her life. Fascinating shit. I didn't know there was so much violence and possessiveness. I'm like, if men tried to restrict women like that, it would look like the Middle East over here. It's amazing, but I could kind of relate to what she was saying because I had witnessed some of that behavior when I lived in Harlem. But her two decades of being a lesbian gave her some interesting insights into the psychology of women, and she was often able to share those insights with me. It also made her a pussy connoisseur where she could look at a woman and know what kind of pussy she had. She could know how wet it would get, if it had a smell or not, and whether the woman was orgasmic. She could tell which women were true lesbians versus those who were faking it or just curious. She would say to me, "I love pussy, Rakhem. I'm not playing around with it when I'm with a woman. I'm eating pussy and expecting my pussy to be eaten right. A lot of women get timid when it's time to get in the bed, but I don't play that. I get it in."

I would sometimes ask her about talking to women when we're out in public. I would say, "How about her? She looks cute, and she looks gay. Would you talk to her?" Monie Love would always say no. She'd say, "I'm not interested in those relationships anymore, Rakhem. They were kind of boring, to be honest, and they were a ton of work. I'd be on the phone and text message all day soothing women and dealing with their emotions. It's just tiring. I mean, I really appreciate the emotional support that I would get when I needed it because women will talk to you all day for weeks to make sure you're ok, but I just can't do that anymore. Plus, I need dick. There's really no comparison between having good dick versus not having it. I need more than to have my pussy eaten. I need to be penetrated by a man. I missed that, and I'm not interested in going back." I could kind of understand what she was saying because men usually come up short when it comes to communicating with women. I know that was the case for me. Women would want to text all fucking day, and I just couldn't keep up. I was only successful with that in two relationships, and that was with Diamond and Bella. I just walked around with the headset in my ear all day, talking to them. Like, we'd talk for eight hours a day every day. But besides the two of them, I just couldn't do it anymore.

She would also criticize certain partners because she said their pussy would throw off the pH of her vagina. "It's not an STD or anything, but one of your partner's pussy doesn't sit well with mine. Every time you go see her and then fuck me, it throws off the pH of my pussy. It's annoying. I just don't like her. I don't really have an issue with any of your partners, Rakhem, but I don't like that about her. That's all I'll say about that." I'm thinking to myself, I'm not really sure what I can do about that. Maybe have that partner do some work around her pH balance or something. The funny thing is the partner that she was criticizing was sexually exclusive with me, so it wasn't like she was picking up anything from anyone else. All I really could do was shrug it off. Monie Love is super sensitive about the STI thing, especially being in the medical industry and treating patients every day. She'd tell me, "I know you have weird beliefs around STIs Rakhem, but be careful out there in these streets. There are a lot of diseases going around. I see it every day." I'm thinking to myself, what are the weird ideas I have around STIs? I've never said anything weird. Do I believe that STIs/STDs exist? Yes, I do. Do I believe that I'm potentially susceptible to STIs? Yes, I do. Do I believe in AIDS as a medical condition? Yes, I do. Do I believe in all the other STIs that are standard? Yes, I do. Do I ever get checked for STIs? Yes, I have. Not sure what's so weird about that. Maybe it's because I don't generally wear condoms with my sexual partners. I used to do that religiously when I was in college, but that was mostly because I was scared of getting someone pregnant.

My thing is I'm only into have real sex, which is both raw and ejaculatory. If a woman and I aren't close enough (or trust each other enough) to have raw sex, then we shouldn't engage in sexual activity. If she wants me to get tested before we have sex, then I'll get tested. No big deal, but I'm not interested in condom sex. It's like jumping into a pool with scuba gear or something. I know I'm in the water, but I wouldn't be able to give you any details about what it feels like. I think my stance on sexuality is considered shocking because I'm honest and upfront about it, but I know people are having raw sex and just not being honest about it. I know folks wear condoms for the first few go-rounds then start going raw soon after. At my age, I'm just not interested in playing games or compromising my pleasure or happiness for someone else's fears or insecurities. And it shouldn't be a problem because there are plenty of people out there who will happily complement whatever your level of sexual safety may be. You can just engage with those people while I engage with mine. I really don't know what else to say about it, but condoms are not my religion. If I'm in a situation where I'm about to have sex and the woman asks me to wear a condom, I'll go ahead and wear it. I've done it a ton of times before, and when I'm requested to wear one, I'm assuming she's trying to protect me, to be honest. I take it as a sign that I should take extra precautions. But will I pursue more sexual activity with her after that? Probably not because it's just not a high-quality sexual experience for me. I feel depleted as a motherfucker, to be honest. It's like I wasn't fed at all like I just masturbated into a bag or something. I literally need to go take a nap after having sex with a condom on and rebuild myself back up. It's bad.

Sex, to me, should be something that feeds the people engaged in it. We should both walk away from that interaction more energized than before we engaged in it. We should feel happier, brighter, and with a better outlook on life. Our stress levels should be lower, and we should be able to think more clearly. That's my experience with sex, and I'm not willing to settle for something less. Again, it's ok to not engage people sexually who you're not aligned with. I do it all the time. It's a part of the sucky part of life to not be able to always get what you want, but it's best to learn to accept that part of life rather than feel resentful of it. That same goes for my relationship philosophy of being open rather than monogamous. There are a lot of women who won't date me because they want something more exclusive than I can offer. Southern Bella refused to engage with me for years because I was dating someone who she thought would take away from the intimacy of our relationship. She wants specialness and intensity and isn't really down with the open relating lifestyle. The only reason she engaged with me the first time was that she thought she would only have to deal with my wife as another woman in my life, but that proved not to be true.

Oh yeah! What about Monie's magnetism? I guess I got caught up in a bunch of tangents. Well, there's something I noticed about Monie Love that created a quandary for me. First of all, she had an absolutely amazing pussy. It was wet and tight and felt like silk. I know I say a lot of my partners have great pussy, and it's true. Part of that is because I make the experience great for myself by allowing myself to feel fully during sex. I allow myself to be vulnerable and feel everything, including the emotions that come up. I've got no problem making any noises, sounds, or faces during sex. I've got no issue with crying if it were to ever come to that. When I was having sex with Erin at her place, her roommate asked her if we were being loud because she was there. She said, "No. We're always loud like that." When Angelina and me used to fuck in hotels, we'd often get noise complaints. It was a fucking mess - sheets wet, phone ringing from the front desk because two motherfuckers wanted to cut the fool. We probably needed a snow cabin on a mountaintop somewhere, to be honest.

But when I say Monie Love had an amazing pussy, I'm saying the box itself had magical qualities. It was the fit of my dick inside her pussy alone that was amazing to me. Later she would tell me that she spends a lot of time cultivating her pussy so that it feels amazing to men when they enter inside of her. She didn't go into those details. Based on the stories she told, I think there is some truth there because I wasn't the only brother who loved how that yoni felt. When Monie Love would visit me after us not seeing each other for a long time, I would damn near die inside of that pussy. Talk about a ninja losing his mind and catching

187

the Holy Ghost. Yeah, that was me. I mean, I wanted to ravage her when I saw her. I couldn't get her to the hotel quick enough. There was something inside of me that wanted her bad as fuck, but I couldn't tell what it was. Monie Love had a beautiful face and was always made up incredibly. Beautiful full lips and the dopest set of eyes on the planet. So beautiful. That said, it's not like her shape was my absolute favorite. She was thick and juicy, and her body felt amazing, but looking at her body didn't whip up my passions for her in the same way that looking into her face did. Her hair was always on point, and her dress was always unique and fashionable. Great style all the way around. She didn't walk sexy, though. She had a regular walk, so it's not like she was pulling me in with feminine wiles, although she was very feminine. So what was it? Well, it took me about four years to figure it out and put words to it.

You see, although I loved the sex that Monie Love and I had, it was hard to be around her for an extended amount of time. When she would come to see me, I would be exhausted after the second day. Day three, I was burnt the fuck out. I had no energy for anything, let alone more sex, or to entertain her or to give her the attention she deserved. I was like, "Why the fuck am I so tired and burnt out?! Why do I want to just crawl up into a hole and hibernate for a week? I need food, sleep, and alone time." I felt so bad about feeling that way, but the lack of energy would affect my ability to hold things together when I was with her. We would get into arguments, and she would think there was something wrong with her or that I didn't like her. But not having any energy made it tough for me to summon patience and consideration for her needs and feelings. It takes energy to "hold space" for a woman's emotions. Like, it's not an automatic thing, and after day three, I was all out of energy. It was the damndest thing.

Fast forward to four years later, and I ended up losing Monie. We didn't break up or anything, but our relationship shifted dramatically. I wasn't able to give her the time, energy, and focus she wanted, which was basically the story of my life. She had mostly been exclusive with me and wanted me to be her primary partner. Instead, she kind of got fed up with things and decided to find other partners who were better suited for her. We were still dating, but our frequency had decreased, and there were some resentful feelings between us. I had told her a few times that I wanted us to spend more time together and that nothing else felt like she did, which was true, but I still couldn't make that happen. The thing was, I would say that when I was in her pussy and she never really trusted what I was saying. She would say, "Rakhem, you're just saying that because you're in this pussy." Later she would tell me, "you be drunk in the pussy" because I would be making all kinds of promises and declarations to her before I ejaculated. I would say all kinds of shit. One day, I was inside of her, and after about ten minutes, I looked down at her face and said, "You're so beautiful, baby." I caressed her face and everything. And she was so incredibly beautiful, but she gave me such a hard time about it later that day. She was cracking up laughing and said, "Rakhem, you should have seen yourself looking into my eyes, calling me beautiful. LMAO. Your mind is gone when you're in this pussy, Rakhem." Maybe my mind is gone, but I think good pussy just brings out my vulnerabilities. It's like alcohol, where it allows me to speak my deepest truths that I otherwise would be afraid to say. The things I was saying to her were all true. But after Monie Love started dating her new partner, she told me some of the observations he made about her. He said that her energy made him want to tear into that pussy. It pulled him way more than he was used to be drawn to a woman and made him want to have sex all the time. He said it was her magnetism. It made him go crazy inside her pussy, yelling and possessing different characters and stuff. He told her it eventually would wear him out to where he needed a break from her. She would ask him what he needed, and he would say, "Time alone." It was amazing that he was able to summarize how I was feeling and put it into words and communicate it to her clearly. After she told me that, I was like, "Yeah, that's exactly how I feel." He told her, "You're just a lot to be around, babe. It's nothing personal at all." That's my thing when Monie Love would come to visit me, we would fuck three times a day, and it was good every time. But then I would eventually get burnt out and need space from her, but at the same time, I wanted to keep fucking. It was the weirdest thing. So when it came time for us to spend more time together, I would try to spend time with her consistently, but then get burnt out the same way whether we were having a lot of sex or not. The thought in my head was, "I need to get out of here" because I felt like I needed to recharge. It was amazing that we were able to have this conversation. She was thinking that I didn't like her or that I was making promises to her that I really didn't mean, but that wasn't the case. Everything I told her was based on how I truly felt. I'm not saying that I didn't overpromise things to her because the reality of how I feel versus what I can truly deliver are two different things. I get that.

Like I said, her magnetism was confusing because looking at her body doesn't necessarily spark a desire within me. Maybe looking into her face or feeling her touch, but not strictly her physical appeal. It was her energy, though. Always pulling me in. Making me want to do for her and engage her and be sexual with her even when I didn't have the internal wherewithal to do it. That was a powerful lesson for me because there are times when it's hard to be around certain people for extended periods of time, but it's not obvious why. Or we mistake their energy for something about their personality. Therefore, we don't take the time to work through how to be together.

When we would have sex, I would feel drained afterward, which wasn't my usual set of feelings following sexual intercourse, but the magnetism explained it. Even while we were having sex, she was still pulling from me. I'm already giving her my physical effort, my focus, my semen, but she was taking my energy at the same time. Like she was sucking my soul into her body as if she were feeding or something. It's not a negative observation. I'm not saying it was an intentionally malicious thing on her part. It's just what it is, and now she's got multiple men who are saying this to her.

## Just like a Friend

Part of my relationship philosophy is that I don't want my partners interacting with each other. If they set things up themselves, then I'm more open to it, but I'm still skeptical like a motherfucker. Before Monie and I started really dating, she hit up Angelina for friendship and advice on how to deal with me. They would become "friends" and talk regularly, but things would go sideways really quickly.

First of all, Angelina would share intimate details of our relationship, including text messages and things I said. All that did was make Monie insecure about her and me. It was a form of torment, actually. It would cause Monie to lash out at me or try to do more in our relationship in order to be accepted by me as measured by what I would do with Angelina. For the longest time, I never knew why Monie was so insecure about us until one day, she told me that Angelina was sharing screenshots of our text messages. Specifically, Angelina showed ones where I talked about how good her pussy was and how much I loved her. I just didn't get that, and it was hard for me to believe at first. Like, why would she even betray our relationship like that?

Later I found out she would kind of rub shit in Monie's face about her situation with me, and that's when I decided I had to move on from her. I don't really know what was going on, but I just didn't want to deal with it anymore. I loved Angelina and valued our relationship, but I couldn't have her impacting my other relationships or adversely impacting Monie's livelihood either. It was time to move on from the relationship and closeness that we had, but I told her we could still fuck here and there. She said that's all she really cared about. Maybe Angelina was just hurt that I was dating Monie, making her lash out like that, but her statement was telling either way.

Much later, I found out that Angelina was coaching Monie on how to have my baby. Like she was literally telling her how to have sex with me in a way that would allow her to have my baby. When I found out about that, I was floored. I was like, "What the entire fuck is that all about?! Why would she even plan and plot some shit out like that knowing that I don't want more children?" I try to not get into people's inner intentions and instead just look at how they treat me. I never did get to the bottom of her intentions, but either way, I can't have that kind of sloppiness around me. Why would I? It just seems self-destructive. So although Angelina and I had an amazing relationship and she showed up for me in so many ways in the past, our time had simply passed. This scenario also solidified the fact that friendships between partners isn't a good thing. I've heard so many stories from my partners about women hitting them up wanting to be friends, but really only wanting information on how to be with me. The shit is scandalous as a moutherfucker. Either way, I'm good on the whole sisterhood, communal thing when it comes to my girlfriends. It's not worth it in the end, and it rarely works out.

## Karen Santiago's Healing Journey

One of the highlights of my open journey was the chance to experience the nurturing from different partners throughout my life. I've always kind of wanted that because I never felt I really had it. And that's a personal feeling and not something that was necessarily representative of the truth. My wife Kenya did a great job of cooking for me for years - two meals a day, taking care of the house, and really doing all the housewife types of duties. She was always available for sex too. But when we started our business, all of that kind of fell off. Kenya got busy with writing her blog and book, which was super dope and kind of put our company on the map. I found myself increasingly taking care of myself and the children more than ever. I would cook for the family, wash dishes, etc., and it all made sense, especially once I stopped working in Corporate America. That said, I still longed for that kind of nurturing. To be honest, I probably didn't feel like I deserved it, especially as an entrepreneur who was no longer bringing in steady paychecks. I remember back at that time even hiring a personal chef, the Tantric Goddess, to make the family meals. She was amazing in the kitchen, but I couldn't afford to keep her for the long term. That was our loss for sure.

It's not just cooking, but also massages, fucking and sucking, head rubs, doing my hair (at least helping me wash it sometimes), checking on me to make sure I'm alright, lying on bosoms, and the like. I don't even really know, to be honest. I just like the idea of being nurtured, and I feel I need it.

So one day, I get a call from Karen Santiago asking if anyone in my men's group would be able to house her for a few months in exchange for her doing some tantric work, massages, and bodywork. I was like, "Ah, me." As a tantric practitioner myself, I was excited to be able to get some of this work done on me for a change. Especially by someone who has actually had some training and that I respect and believe in. Karen Santiago got her tantra training from one of my old associates who has spent just as much time as me doing energy work and teaching others. Plus, she told me she had worked out a similar arrangement with one of the brothers in my men's group already, and it went well.

I had met Karen Santiago before, according to her, but I didn't remember it. Apparently, she came to my house and stayed a few days with Kenya, but I was out of town with one of my other girlfriends. We did get to meet, though. Seeing her again when I picked her up from the bus station was like my first time. She was tall, heavyset, with a beautiful face and hair. I think what stood out the most about her were her beautiful thick lips, expertly painted, and her eyes. She was always very sweet and soft-spoken with a high voice that kind of made my dick hard every time I heard it. I couldn't place my finger on what it was about her voice that sounded so appealing, but it was something. Her voice seemed partially contrived as if she had some kind of voice training through acting lessons, but it still sounded really nice.

We got to my house, and Karen Santiago was eager to get started on doing some work on me, but I wasn't feeling any urgency. It helped me understand that part of my problem in not getting the nurturing I needed from partners was my own personal resistance to it. She wanted to work on me four or five times a week, but it ended up being only four or five times total during the three months she stayed. That was all on me. But by day three, we were able to get some table work in. She was able to do energy work and some bodywork on me. It went really well, and I appreciated it. I felt nurtured and cared for. She also took the time to cook for me and bring me plates of food. She kept the bedroom spotless, plus she had an oil dispenser unit that had the room smelling all herbal and fresh. That was great. I think she even did my laundry, but I can't exactly remember. I do all my own laundry because I don't want my clothes to get mixed in with my children's or to be washed the wrong way and ruined.

NOTE: Not sure if I mentioned this or not, but I live in the same house as Kenya, but we have our own bedrooms. Whenever I have partners come over, they can just stay in the room with me.

So, yes, Karen Santiago delivered on her promise to do bodywork and nurture me, but let's be honest, she also wanted to fuck me. I mean, when she moved into the house, she wasn't my partner or anything, but somehow we would get into these conversations where we would discuss the requirements for being my girlfriend. She'd ask, "So, Rakhem, how does a woman become your girlfriend? Is there something they need to do to get that title?" My response was kind of guarded because I knew she was really asking how she could be my girlfriend. I'm not sure what I think about these women sometimes. It's like I'm in denial about what they really want. Like, when she asked to come and stay a couple of months, I didn't even consider that she actually wanted to be one of my partners. I can see Monie Love slapping her own forehead now at my complete and utter stupidity when it comes to women. I can see her saying, "Rakhem, how can you not know that these women want to be with you. And on top of that, they want to be number one in your life." I guess I am naive sometimes.

When Karen Santiago asked me about the qualifications to become a girlfriend, I just said, "Well, it really depends on what the woman wants compared to what I want. Like, if we like each other, she's clear that I won't be exclusive with her, talk to her regularly, or ever leave my wife, and that I'll be doing what I want to do with my time, then I guess she can be my girlfriend." The long and short of it was, she became my girlfriend. What's even more interesting is that she actually suggested on multiple occasions that we should be exclusive with one another. That was amazing to me, considering that she was newly in my life. Sometimes I'm amazed by a woman's boldness. It's like I have thirty girlfriends and a wife, but you think we should be sexually exclusive? It's not that I'm against sexual exclusivity, but the question is, "Why would I do that?" What's the advantage to me of no longer fucking almost any woman I want whenever I want? Why would I give up total and complete freedom and autonomy just to be beholden to one person with complex needs, emotional hang-ups, and more than likely (based on the desire to be exclusive) self-esteem issues?

But this gets into the crux of the story. What I realized over time is that Karen Santiago had major hang-ups about her sexuality due to some earlier traumas that she hadn't yet resolved. Her ideology was that love and sex was a sacred and special thing that should only be afforded to a very special few throughout a lifetime. As a result, she was super selective in terms of who she would date or interact with. In other words, she wasn't really able to date freely and openly. She didn't trust men. She didn't trust herself, and she wasn't able to attract the quality of love and partnership she desired. That may sound extreme, but a lot of people (male and female) find themselves in the same predicament. They find themselves in hurtful relationships or with sexually incompatible people. I don't judge them or their relationships. Still, they have a problem finding the god or goddess within to best manifest their lives. It is about releasing judgment of your past and living in the present. It is about realizing that you only attract who and what you are and therefore all is in alignment. It's about understanding that you're not a victim in life and that the world isn't out there full of villains chomping at the bit to take advantage of you. My goal in life is to attempt to live in the abundance of love in all my relationships, so I don't subscribe to the scarcity ideology.

Another important thing to realize about me is that I'm what I call the low hanging fruit when it comes to relationships. What I mean is that everyone can get along with me really easily. I'm easy to talk to. I'm polite, funny, interesting, and intelligent. I'm aware of my surroundings and empathetic to whatever you might be going through. I'm a confident person who's not afraid to speak his mind, but I'm not arrogant. So, of course, Karen Santiago is going to feel safe talking to me and being with me, but I'm not here to be exclusive with you. You can't just take the easy way out and settle down with Rakhem Seku. I'm here to support you in getting over your trauma so you can attract the love you really desire. To move you out of victimhood into something more empowering. In other words, I'm just a bridge to get you from point A to point B. I'm not the final destination. My life mission and philosophy are totally different from the average person. I live and love in a tantric way; meaning, I come from an abundance theory of love, which is why I have so many girlfriends.

Everyone I have sex with is a lovemaking experience for me. I love them, and they love me. PERIOD! Love isn't scarce or hard to find. It's abundant, which is how it's supposed to be. That's the tantric way. I only attract myself and my compliment, so I can't really go wrong with those I'm drawn to and those drawn to me. Some people hide behind the guise of being "selective" when, in fact, they have fears, insecurities, and various hang-ups about themselves and their sexuality. You don't have to practice being selective because, as human beings, we're naturally selective. It's called attraction. That's your selection antenna. If you have knowledge and understanding, then it's your ultimate guide. If you're still working through fears, it becomes your nemesis and something to be judged. I only attract amazing people who are divine and beautiful and have my best interest at heart or who have something to teach me. That's the tantric way.

I've often said that those who have gone through the most trauma often provide the most intense sexual connections. I think that was true with Karen Santiago. The sex was really, really god. Her pussy stayed wet and she had an exceptional head game. She knew how to get me to the edge of wanting to come without letting me. She was intuitive in that way. I had to tell her a few times, "Just let me come damn it. Fuck!!" She was highly skilled sexually and really knew what she was doing. She also could squeeze her vagina really tight to where I couldn't penetrate her any deeper than I was. It was like an advanced kegel technique. I've been with a lot of women that could kegel their vagina, but all they could do was apply additional pressure on my lingam. I could still move it freely as I needed to, but that wasn't the case with Karen Santiago. When she clamped that pussy closed that was it. No further entry. A few times. I thought I hit the bottom of the pussy when, in reality, I was stopped by the pressure of two walls coming together. It really was profound. I asked her about it one day and she told me it was just her squeezing. I was like, "Fuck!!" But she also said it happens without her knowing it sometimes, which is equally amazing to me.

What didn't I like about the sex? She wasn't on any birth control, and I wasn't sure of her cycle tracking abilities. That shit made me nervous as a motherfucker. I don't care how wet the pussy is; if I can't come in it freely, then we have a problem. For me, it's like the sex act is incomplete. Plus, she still wanted to have children because she didn't have any yet, and I'm like, "Nah." Let me play things safe here and protect my legacy.

Since our time together, I've encouraged her to branch out and connect with some of the men who've shown interest in dating her. I'm not saying all of them are solid brothers, but some of them seem sincere in their desire to connect with her in a holistic and caring manner. She's a powerful woman, so I know that she'll be able to create and navigate these dating waters with no problem. I also know that, once she gets over some of her past traumas, she'll attract a man that's just as powerful as she is.

## Gia's Worship

"Namaste" means I see the god in you. But my question is, do you really see the god in me? If you saw God, how would you react? It really sounds more like you see god as a human rather than seeing this human as god.

Gia saw god in me, and she declared it to the world. I loved that because it made her declaration seem more real to me. Think about it, if you're a Christian and you saw Jesus walking down the street, how would you react? Would you announce it to the world and let people know? I'm pretty sure there would be some excitement happening. That's how Gia was with me. She let the world know she saw god in me and exactly how it impacted her life. She created pictures, monuments, and narratives around my godhood, and I have to admit, it helped me feel better about my potential to be great in all ways.

Everyone needs a Gia in their life, and I'm happy to have her in my life.

# ~ 4 ~
## Epilogue

# Epilogue

No one is against me. My experiences are my own creation. I live without regret, and I continue to learn and grow into my most divine potential. I'm thankful for my life and everyone who has contributed to it, regardless of whether those interactions were pleasurable or hurtful. I know that all of the women in my life are my reflection and have contributed to me becoming a better man. I know that all of the women I've related with over the years were doing the absolutely best they could. I know that I was also doing the best I could as well. I harbor no blame towards anyone in my life - past, present, or future. I was never a victim, nor was I the villain. In all ways, I worked to stay present in my life creations and relationships, but sometimes I did run from the reflection of myself. I loved all of the women I related with without exception. Even the ones who triggered the hurt within me. I know that I was perceived as the villain in many of my relationships, but I don't accept that label. That said, I do acknowledge being the trigger for hurt, pain, and lessons for some of women I've dated over the decades. This, too, is a part of my growth. It counters the story I've created for myself of being the good boy and the one to never hurt women in the same way that my biological father hurt my mother. I know that I had to interact with many women who were ultimately the triggers for my healing in order to wake up to the truth of myself. To all of them, I say, "Thank you for being the vessel of enlightenment and awakening for me."

The love and appreciation I have for my mother has grown over the years. I understand her pain as well as her desire to see the absolute best in me. I've learned to accept her offering of love for both my brother and me. I've learned to connect with her as a friend and not just a son. I've grown to appreciate all that she's given me that makes me a unique and talented being on this planet. I've seen her reflection in many of the women I've dated, and that has allowed me to love her more, just as it has allowed me to love myself more. I am a part of her. I am a continuation of her legacy as a spiritual human being. I also appreciate my biological father for all he has given me and taught me about life. He was the one who taught me the truth of marriage and women and how to honor your desires as a man. I understand his choices and accept them and love him without condition. I love my father as well for demonstrating to me what unconditional love in action really looks like. For being that example of manhood and what it means to have an edge. I thank my mother and father for showing me what decades of dedicated love and commitment look like inside a relationship and marriage. I thank Kenya for being the perfect reflection and partner to allow me to grow into my best self.

This is my story.

The Progressive Love Academy (PLA) is your #1 relationship tools and information resource online school on the web for creating your life and ideal relationship. No other online relationship school has the number of tools, resources, and certification courses.

With courses and certifications like:

- UPLVL Communications™ Certification
- The Relationship Tools Video Library
- The Trust Forum
- The Three Way Mirror Certification Course
- Feminine Power 101
- The Blue Butterfly Women's Empowerment
- The Peaceful Warrior Men's Development

For more information go to

https://www.progressiveloveacademy.com

# The Art of Open
# Relating: Volume 1~
## *Theory, Philosophy, & Foundation*

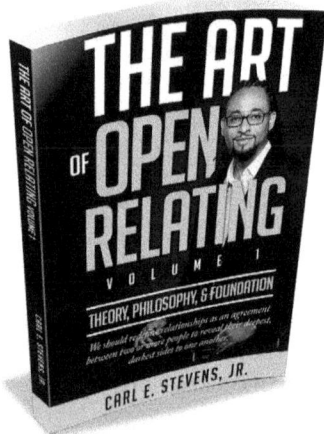

Continue your learning experience by reading *The Art of Open Relating: Volume 1: Theory, Philosophy, & Foundation* to expand your knowledge of open relating and alternative styles to love. Examine the additional relationship styles available and determine if a freedom-based relating model is right for you.

*Available on Amazon*

# UPLVL Communication:
## *The Ultimate Solution to Save Relationships and Eliminate Hurtful, Damaging, & Meaningless Arguments*

We finally have a solution to bring couples closer together in LOVE and not further apart in hurt. UPLVL Communication™ is the premier communication system for leaving absolutely no doubt about what your partner is saying, why they're saying it, how to respond to them with love and compassion, and what they're looking for on the deepest levels. Finally, understand WHO is speaking and get to the very source of the trigger, conflict, and pain points that would otherwise go unaddressed. It's time to close the communication gap, once and for all. Kenya and Carl Stevens are the founders of the Progressive Love™ Academy, the premier school for relationships and personal empowerment. Their tools and coaching have saved countless marriages and empowered thousands to live their absolute best life.

*Available on Amazon*

# Finding Male Sexuality:
## *My Personal Journey in Awakening the Masculine Sexual Self*

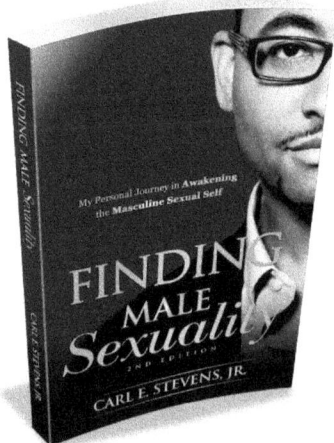

Continue your learning experience by reading the second edition of *Finding Male Sexuality: My Personal Journey in Awakening the Masculine Sexual Self.* This book illustrates many of my sexual experiences that were critical in awakening my sexual power and skill as an effective lover to my many partners. Part 2 of the book gives practical exercises any man can use to awaken his sexual mastery.

*Available on Amazon*

# Tame Your Woman:
## *Become the Man She Needs*

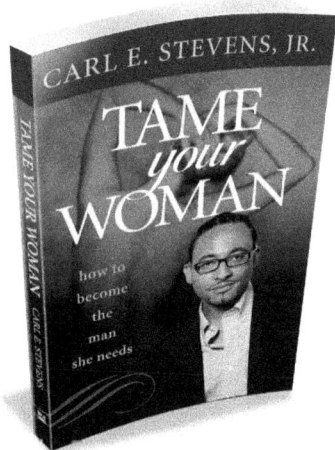

How do you have a relationship with a woman who pees standing up? That was the question Carl had to ask himself after marrying fiery, young Kenya, whose need for dominance and control overshadowed not only his needs but her abilities. There were a lot of broken lamps in the early years of their relationship. There were moments when things teetered on the edge of getting a lot uglier than a broken lamp, too. Thankfully, a radical change in attitude saved their marriage. They became strong enough to thrive through big challenges: parenthood, losing their home to fire, and Kenya's near-fatal illness. Carl, who now co-leads relationship workshops with Kenya, shares the lessons learned not only from his own struggle to be in a relationship of equals but also from deep study Kenya and he have done on the subject. In this book, readers will learn: --Why "a boy cannot become a man until he has healed a woman." —How to determine what a woman really wants, and how to give it to her without losing your self-respect or her respect for you. --Why your position on the "Monk Scale" makes all the difference to your success as a husband and father. --How to keep your own vices from getting in the way of your relationship.

*Available on Amazon*

# Manifesting Marriage for Women:
# WORKBOOK

*9 Steps to Finding Your Partner and Creating
a Successful Marriage*

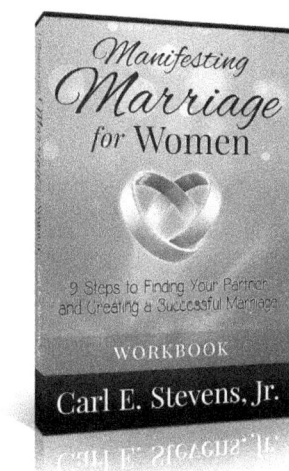

The *Manifesting Marriage for Women* workbook is designed to assist women in finding their life partner and create a long term successful marriage. The steps are easy to follow and provide assignments to guide you through the process.

*Available on Amazon*

# Change Your Man:
## *How to Become the Woman He Wants*

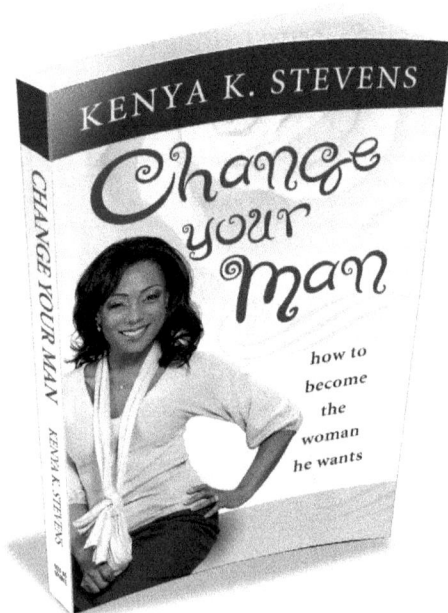

Learn the secrets of femininity and how to find true love in your life. Attract the man of your dreams by learning to change the inner you. Don't allow your inner man to stop you from attracting the man you've always desired. In this book, Kenya K. Stevens discusses the secrets she used to attract her husband and find true love.

*Available on Amazon*